Plan & Go | Trans-Catalina & Backbone Trails

All you need to know to complete two long-distance trails through Southern California's coastal Mediterranean climate

Sam Ward

sandiburg press

Plan & Go | Trans-Catalina & Backbone Trails

All you need to know to complete two long-distance trails through
Southern California's coastal Mediterranean climate

Published by sandiburg press
www.sandiburgpress.com

SAFETY NOTICE: This book describes physically challenging activities in remote outdoor environments which carry an inherent risk of personal injury or death. While the author(s) and sandiburg press have made every effort to ensure that the information contained herein was accurate at the time of publication, they are not liable for any damage, injury, loss, or inconvenience arising directly or indirectly from using this book. Your safety and health during preparations and on the trail are your responsibility. This book does not imply that any of the trails described herein are appropriate for you. Make sure you fully understand the risks, know your own limitations, and always check trail conditions as they can change quickly.

Content

Welcome

Within these pages, you will find the information needed to carefully prepare for and confidently thru-hike two of Southern California's newest and most unique hiking trails, the Trans-Catalina Trail on Santa Catalina Island and the Backbone Trail in the Santa Monica Mountains.

You will find essential backpacking information including details on campsites, water sources, resupply points, access points, permits, popular section hikes, fitness requirements and training, planning tips, and suggested gear as well as an overview of the biology you may encounter along the way. I have backpacked both trails twice and will provide suggestions based on my personal experience as well as a day-by-day account of my hikes.

The Trans-Catalina Trail (TCT) and the Backbone Trail (BBT) provide a unique opportunity to backpack while surrounded by both mountain and ocean views. The notoriously "perfect" weather of Southern California should make for pleasant hiking and provide an opportunity to experiment with lightweight backpacking gear. The rare Mediterranean climate and ecosystems of both trails will make you forget you are only miles from the conveniences and culture of the second-largest city in the United States, Los Angeles.

Catalina Conservancy Sign with Mount Orizaba in the Back

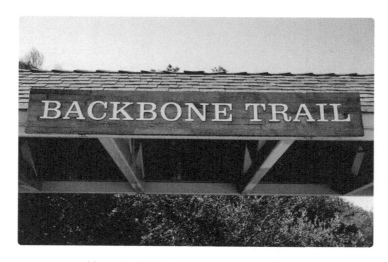

Backbone Trail Sign at Kanan Dume Road Trailhead

< Welcome >

Introduction

Both the Trans-Catalina Trail and the Backbone Trail have a history of use as routes through the mountains. But officially, they have only been established in recent years as complete end-to-end routes. The Trans-Catalina Trail pieces together fire roads and access roads to Santa Catalina's interior to create the route across the island. The Backbone Trail has existed in sections for decades as part of a network of trails through the Santa Monica Mountains and was finally completed as a continuous route in 2016.

The Trans-Catalina Trail

Santa Catalina Island emerged from the Pacific Ocean about one to two million years ago as a result of tectonic plate motion associated with the San Andreas Fault. Catalina Island did not become separated from the mainland due to sea level rise. It has been an island for its entire existence. The first inhabitants of the island were the Tongva people, who came over from established mainland villages and settled the island around seven thousand years ago. They primarily harvested the sea for food and traded extensively with the mainland. One of their famous exports were bowls and cookware carved out of soapstone, which were distributed throughout the southwest U.S. along trading routes. One of the soapstone quarries can be visited right on the TCT near the airport.

The Spanish eventually "discovered" the island in 1542 and, by the early 1800s, had relocated all the native people to missions on the mainland. Spain did not have a strong presence on the island, so hunters, trappers, and smugglers moved in to fill the void left behind after the removal of the native population. The many coves along the island's coastline provided shelter for these uninvited visitors. Catalina Island was briefly part of Mexico after their independence from Spain in 1821 and then became a part of the U.S. in 1848 after the Mexican-American War. Ranchers and prospectors started to inhabit the island, beginning the slow destruction of the island's ecology, which had developed over the million years or so since it rose from the sea.

During the Civil War, Union soldiers were stationed on the island to remove the ranchers and prospectors, who might side with the Confederates, as well as to determine if the island was suitable for internment of Native Americans during the war. The army barracks are now the maroon Isthmus Yacht Club building in Two Harbors, right on the TCT. By the turn of the 20th century, the island had become a vacation destination. Ownership changed hands many times before William Wrigley Jr., of Wrigley chewing gum, took over and heavily developed the island as a resort and hotel destination, even bringing the Chicago Cubs over for spring training. In 1975, the Wrigley family deeded 88 percent of the island to the Catalina Island Conservancy. The Conservancy has been actively working to reverse the ecological damage of past generations by promoting native species and removing harmful invasive species.

The first documented traverse of Catalina Island was by Thad Jones, Steve Royce, and Dick Lyon in 1956. The story goes that they jumped into the ocean from a ship off the east end of the island, scaled the cliffs up to the top of the island, then jogged and bushwhacked their way to the west end. From there, they jumped back into the ocean and climbed onto their boat, all within 11 hours and 20 minutes. Today, there is a network of trails and roads used to access the island's interior that the TCT follows to create an east-to-west route. The TCT was officially opened in 2009 and invites people to take on the same challenge that Thad, Steve, and Dick did back in 1956.

The Backbone Trail

The Santa Monica Mountains were formed by tectonic collisions along the San Andreas Fault. They are part of the Transverse Ranges of Southern California, named for their unusual east-west orientation. Predecessors of the Chumash people occupied the mountains beginning somewhere around 7,000 to 9,000 years ago. Early settlements formed at the lagoons and estuaries where mountain streams emptied into the Pacific Ocean. The native people gathered nuts from the forest and eventually started fishing and hunting with enough proficiency to expand the population and become well-established in the region. The Chumash culture became more defined a few thousand years ago, and their territory spanned the western portion of the range, including settlements in what is now Malibu Creek State Park. The eastern portion of the range was occupied by the Tongva people of the Los Angeles Basin.

Once the Spanish began settling California heavily in the mid to late 1700s, the native people were forced into missions and their presence in the mountains faded. The Spanish eventually lost control of California when Mexico declared independence. After the Mexican-American War, California became part of the United States. The first census of Los Angeles recorded 141 people in 1841. For the next few decades, Los Angeles would be on a steady pace of growth, as Americans moved west in search of gold, oil, and a new way of life. It was only within the last 100 years that it started the path towards a sprawling urban region, spawned by transporting water hundreds of miles from the Sierra Nevada. Today, the Santa Monica Mountains are surrounded by one of the most populous areas in the country and face immense pressure from development and human impact.

The Backbone Trail has been a vision for decades, but private land ownership made a route through the mountains difficult. Slowly but surely state and federal agencies expanded park lands and acquired easements and access rights from private landowners. For years, the BBT existed as patches of trails with no way to connect all the sections for a complete thru-hike. In 2016, the last crucial pieces of land were gifted to the National Park Service, including a donation by former governor Arnold Schwarzenegger, that established a continuous route through the mountains and completed the dream of the BBT. The official end-to-end route was dedicated and announced as a National Recreation Trail during a ceremony on June 4, 2016.

Over the next few years, the National Park Service and California State Parks as well as the Santa Monica Mountains Conservancy and Mountains Recreation Conservancy Authority will work together to develop and implement a comprehensive Trail Management Plan for the Santa Monica Mountains that would include, among many other elements of a trail network, development of new backcountry camps for both equestrians and hikers along the Backbone Trail. The Santa Monica Mountains National Recreation Area Interagency Trail Management Plan has been drafted but must undergo an environmental review, public comment period, final evaluation of alternatives, and then acquire funding before any work can begin. That said, it will most likely be several years from the publication date of this book before ground is broken on these camps. In the meantime, the information in this guidebook will get·you through the challenges of planning a thru-hike along the BBT.

In summary, the interior of Catalina Island and the Santa Monica Mountains are geological and ecological marvels best enjoyed from ground level at a walking pace. Explore wilderness areas few people ever see. Wake up next to bobcats and bison. Walk through a field of wildflowers. Feel the ocean breeze from a mountain peak. The joy of thru-hiking is immersing yourself in these regions and witnessing the transitions from night to day, from sea to hilltop, from grassland to woodland, first-hand and uninterrupted. This guidebook was written to provide you with all the information you need to create your own continuous journey through these rare and beautiful environments and forge memories that last a lifetime.

Figure 1 – Overview Map of Trans-Catalina & Backbone Trails

These routes are fun. They are challenging, but not dangerous. This book summarizes all the pertinent and current information available on these recently-established trails. The following chapter, Chapter 1, summarizes the challenges to expect on both trails as well as time and budget requirements for an overview of what a multi-day trip along the two routes might require. Chapters 2 and 3 present details on the Trans-Catalina Trail and the Backbone Trail, respectively, including trail and weather conditions, camping options, water sources, points of interest, flora and fauna, as well as potential safety hazards. Chapter 4 covers advanced planning, including specific travel options for accessing each trail, to ensure your preferred arrangements will be available. Chapter 5 presents itinerary, food, resupply, and training recommendations, while Chapter 6 makes gear suggestions specific to these trails. The final chapter, Chapter 7, is a personal account of my experience planning and hiking these two trails, including a day-by-day journal of my hikes. I hope this book provides you with enough detail to pick and choose the components that work for you and create your own one-of-a-kind hiking experience.

Visit *www.PlanAndGoHiking.com* for more information and pictures.

1. Summary of the Challenge

While the TCT and BBT each offer a backpacking experience like no other, you must earn it. Climbing from sea level to thousands of feet in the air under the blazing sun will test your will. The following chapter goes over the physical challenges, time required, and budget you should expect to complete these trails.

a. Requirements

Neither trail requires any specialized or technical gear, but there are some unique challenges involved. The hot and dry weather of Southern California combined with extensive sun-exposed sections of trail make hiking very strenuous at times. The TCT especially lacks shade, and the climbs are at a very steep grade in some sections. If you have not experienced hot, exposed, dry-weather backpacking, the effort may be a bit of a shock. Seriously consider avoiding summer months unless you are very comfortable hiking in these environments.

In addition to the environmental challenges, both trails present significant logistical challenges. The TCT is entirely on an island, so you must coordinate your travel to the island with your hiking itinerary. The BBT has sparse official campsites and water sources, which significantly alter your daily mileages.

You should be able to hike at least 10 miles in one day to do the TCT and 10-15 miles per day to do the BBT. The longest distance to a campground on the TCT is 15.7 miles. The BBT has one 20-mile stretch between convenient camping options. There are off-trail options, presented in Chapters 2 and 3, to alter the hikes somewhat and shorten those long stretches between camping. Don't let big mileages intimidate you. You may not know exactly how many miles you can cover in a day until you attempt them on the trail. That's the fun of a challenge!

One of the great benefits of these trails is their mild climate, which is perfect for lightweight backpacking. If the miles required are outside of your comfort range, consider that you could be hauling less gear than what you're used to.

b. Time

Both the TCT and the BBT only allow camping at designated campgrounds, so the number of days it will take is largely influenced by the camping constraints. Not all the campgrounds are spaced out evenly. Some days may be very long to reach the next campground while other days only require a short distance. If you are a strong hiker you will be able to skip some campgrounds. Look at the campground descriptions and distances in Sections 2d (TCT) and 3d (BBT) to get a feel for the campgrounds you desire and if they are within a comfortable distance from each other. These trails are not extremely long, so, if your schedule allows, you could spend a night at each campground and really stretch your time out on the trail.

The time it takes you to hike these trails depends on your goals for the hike. It can be an aggressive three-day, or even two-day, hike or a leisurely week-long trip. Both styles work great for these trails but don't expect to hike them faster than two days, unless you are running, and any slower than seven days, unless you take days off along the way. The climbing on the TCT is much more strenuous than on the BBT so keep that in mind when looking at daily mileages.

The daily mileage required to hike each trail within two to seven days is shown in the table below.

	2 days	3 days	4 days	5 days	6 days	7 days
TCT (51.4 miles)	25.7	17.1	12.9	10.3	8.6	7.3
BBT (72.8 miles)	36.4	24.3	18.2	14.6	12.1	10.4

Table 1 – Average Daily Mileages based on Planned Trail Days

The actual mileage may vary by several miles for both trails depending on off-trail camping used and route decisions. The total trail mileage shown is conservative and includes additional mileage likely required to access the eastern and western terminuses of the TCT (13.9 miles) as well as campgrounds along the BBT (6 miles). Consult the suggested itineraries and mileage data tables in the appendix for a more accurate look at your daily mileage. As you can see, there is not a huge difference in the daily miles required to hike the trails in five or six days. The difference there could be made up by a morning versus an afternoon start on the first day.

Your schedule may float between a few different estimates of days, but, luckily, there are no permit systems that require setting hard dates for your hike. You can adjust your estimate without much consequence as you research more into the hike and discover interesting areas where you want to spend more time. The biggest issue that could arise is that campsites may be booked on days you want to switch to. Check availability early online once you have a date in mind, especially if you are hiking in the busy season (May through September).

I have hiked the TCT and BBT twice each, both times taking different approaches to the hike. The first time, I did aggressive mileage and hiked the TCT in three days and the BBT in about two days. When I hiked them the second time, I spent five days on the TCT and four on the BBT but could have easily spent a fifth day on the BBT had my schedule allowed. Based on those experiences, I would say five days is a good starting point for planning and adjust that as you learn more about the trails.

c. Budget

Trans-Catalina Trail

Your main expenses for the TCT will be the ferry ticket ($72 round trip) and camping, which varies depending on the campground and season, ranging from $14 to $26 per night. Summer rates are higher. There is also a $9.25 reservation fee per campsite, which you could split if multiple people were staying at the same campsite. You also will likely need a water delivery to Parsons' Landing ($20), since that is the only campground on the west side of the island and there is no water there. The water delivery includes firewood and a firestarter log.

The expenses listed above are the minimum you will pay if you want to hike the length of the TCT. Additional expenses are parking at the ferry port ($17/day) and food purchased at restaurants on the island. The table below shows expected costs for one person to hike for four days on the TCT:

Expense Item	Total Cost
$68 travel to ferry (ride service or $17 parking x 4 days)	$68
$72 ferry	$72
$22 camping/person/night x 3 nights	$66
$9.25 fee/campground x 3 campgrounds	$28
$20 for water at Parsons' Landing	$20
Permits	FREE
Total for four days	**$254**
Average daily expense	**$63.50**

Table 2 – Expected Expenses for Hiking the TCT

The camping and ferry fees are a little steep compared to standard rates around the country, but consider that you are getting a world-class vacation and hiking experience for four days at $63.50 a day.

The above cost estimate does not include additional lodging at Avalon or Two Harbors if you want to spend some extra days on the island before or after the trail. It also does not include costs of food, fuel, or island transportation services, such as shuttles or gear hauling services. Hiking with a partner or group would allow for sharing of the $9.25 camping fee, the Parsons' Landing water delivery (2 people can split one water delivery), and any transportation or parking costs to the ferry ports.

An additional consideration is to become a Catalina Island Conservancy member for $35. You will receive 50% off camping fees (but not the $9.25 reservation fee) for all campgrounds except Two Harbors and Hermit Gulch, which are not on Conservancy land. The Catalina Flyer ferry, which only travels between Newport Beach and Avalon, is offering 50% off ferry tickets for Conservancy members. Members also get free admission for the Wrigley Memorial and Botanical Gardens near Hermit Gulch Campground (not on the TCT but an alternate near Avalon). Most importantly, you would be helping support the organization that not only created and maintains the TCT but does outstanding conservation work for the delicate island ecology.

Backbone Trail

Your main expenses for the BBT will be the camping fees, which range from $7 to $45 per night. Additional expenses are parking at the trailheads ($8/day) or travel to the trailheads. The table below shows expected costs for one person to hike for five days on the BBT:

Expense Item	Total Cost
$40 travel to trailhead (ride service or $8 parking x 5 days)	$40
$25 camping/person/night x 4 nights	$100
Permits	FREE
Total for five days	**$140**
Average daily expense	**$28**

Table 3 – Expected Expenses for Hiking the BBT

Make sure to carry exact change if you will be staying at Musch Trail Camp ($7), because payment is done through an envelope system and there is no way to get change back. Also, if you will be staying at Cleft of the Rock Ranch, or anyone's private home, it is always good to show your appreciation with cash even though they may never mention money to you.

2. What to Expect – Trans-Catalina Trail

You've just finished an exhilarating climb along an exposed ridgeline with sweeping ocean views the whole way. The climb started from a serene private beach, where, during an extended stop for lunch, you took a dip in the cool, clear Pacific Ocean. The sweat covering your face meets a strong gust of wind and now that same ocean you gazed out at during lunch is over a thousand feet below you. You catch your breath while observing the rugged island coastline ahead of you then march out towards afternoon beers at the Two Harbors village. Welcome to the Trans-Catalina Trail! This chapter provides you with a picture of the conditions, campsites, water sources, and points of interests along the route as well suggestions for gear and hiking schedule to enjoy everything the TCT has to offer.

a. Trails & Navigation

The TCT is officially listed as 37.2 miles from end to end, but if you want to walk every step of the trail, you will most likely end up walking 51.4 miles. Both the eastern and western terminuses of the trail are several miles from the closest ferry terminal, so be prepared for extra walking at both the start and end of the hike. The western terminus of the TCT is a rocky remote beach with no available transportation services and the eastern terminus is almost a 2-mile road walk outside the city of Avalon from the ferry dock. These "extra" miles make the trip longer than advertised, but, fortunately, they are somewhat easy miles without significant elevation gain. There are also some options for alternative routes that can reduce backtracking or shortcut sections if you are on a tight schedule.

Hiking Direction

Your hiking direction can be influenced by several factors on the TCT. The biggest constraint will be the ferry schedules at Avalon or Two Harbors. If you want to hike a big first or final day, keep the schedule in mind and make sure you give yourself enough time to hike all those miles and still make it to the ferry. Ferries in and out of Avalon are much more frequent, so if you have a tight travel window on one end of the trip, Avalon will provide you with the most flexibility.

Outside of your own travel schedule, there are only small differences between a westbound (WB) and an eastbound (EB) hike. The western portion of the island, west of the Two Harbors isthmus, is much more remote. If you would like to transition into more solitude as your hike progresses, WB is the way to go. Avalon in the east offers many more amenities. If you want to end your hike where you have access to restaurants, bars, and hotels, then EB would work for you. The mile markers along the trail are oriented in the WB direction so that seems to be the recommended direction of the Catalina Island Conservancy, the organization that administers the trail and owns most of the land it crosses.

One other factor to consider is the almost 16 miles from the Avalon ferry terminal to the first campsite, Blackjack Campground. If you will be hiking WB, this is the first stretch of trail and, considering most ferries don't get into Avalon until 10:00 AM or later, it may be difficult to cover the 16 miles before sunset. (There is one ferry from Long Beach that arrives at 7:00 AM and is recommended for WB hikers.) Consider staying at Hermit Gulch Campground just outside of Avalon, but off the TCT, to help break up this distance and also cut 5 miles off the hike to Blackjack Campground.

Trail Conditions

Trail conditions are generally good along the TCT. The trail is mostly well-marked at intersections and has convenient mile markers along the route (counting up going in the WB direction) to help you track your progress. The route mostly follows seldom-traveled dirt roads across the island with a few miles of single-track trail scattered throughout. The roads and trails can be extremely steep in some sections, making the climbs and descents tiring and longer to complete. Keep this in mind when planning your days out as you may be slowed down a bit by some of these steep sections.

Figure 2 – Dirt Road Walking | Typical Shade Structure

The highest elevations on the TCT may give the sense that it is an easy trail, but consider that you must reach those heights starting at sea level, several times. Those climbs and descents can be exhilarating but strenuous. Take a look at the elevation profile in Figure 3 below, and you will not find many stretches of flat trail, the exception being the recommended off-TCT return route to Two Harbors from Parsons' Landing along West End Road.

The most difficult aspect of the trail may be staying cool and comfortable in the continuous sun exposure. When constant sun exposure is combined with sparse water sources and steep climbs, the difficulty ramps up significantly. If you see any shade, no matter how small, take the opportunity to rest there if you need it, as there may not be another shady spot for miles. There are a few shade structures along the trail at convenient rest spots. Those structures are indicated on the map and elevation profile in Appendix B.

- **Highest point:** The TCT reaches an elevation of 1,765' just before the trail begins its steep descent to Parsons' Landing. Mt. Orizaba (2,097 ft.), Blackjack Mountain (2,010 ft.), and Silver Peak (1,804 ft.) are all higher and easily accessed from the TCT.

- **Lowest point:** Any of the beaches, all at sea level. Avalon, Little Harbor, Two Harbors, Parsons' Landing, and Starlight Beach are all at or close to sea level, where the TCT passes them.

- **Steepest decline/ascent:** There are many very steep portions of the TCT, but the most sustained occur on the trail approaching Silver Peak from Two Harbors and Parsons' Landing. The section between Parsons' Landing and the junction with the Silver Peak Trail is one of the steepest you may come across on any trail, changing 900 feet in 0.8 miles. Between Two Harbors and the Silver Peak Trail, the TCT gains 1,260 feet in 1.4 miles from the start of the climb out of Two Harbors to Water Tank Road.

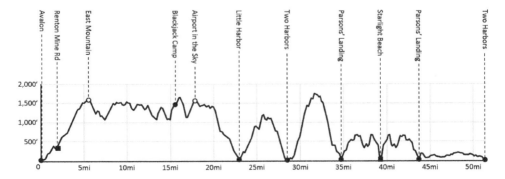

Figure 3 – Elevation Profile of the TCT

Trail Access

Hiking across an island is an amazing backpacking opportunity. Unfortunately, this makes trail access complicated. The primary access points are via ferry to Avalon and Two Harbors. Private charter boats, planes, and helicopter rides to the island are also available if you can afford it. Otherwise, plan on taking the ferry.

There are also options for getting around the island once you have arrived from the mainland if you want to start or end your hike somewhere other than the ferry ports. For details on ferries and island transportation services check out Section 4c *Travel Arrangements*.

Two Harbors

Walk southwest out of the town center along the eucalyptus-lined road starting at the bathroom facilities. When you reach the maroon Isthmus Yacht Club building, take the following trail depending on your direction:

Westbound (to Parsons' Landing) – Head west on Banning House Road, then turn immediately southwest along the western shore of the harbor, opposite of where the ferries come in. Continue southwest on level ground for 0.7 miles before heading west and starting the long climb up to Silver Peak.

Eastbound (to Avalon) – Head east on Banning House Road, continue uphill past the Banning House.

Avalon

Finding the trailhead is a bit trickier from Avalon. The true trailhead starts almost a 2-mile walk outside of Avalon at the intersection of Wrigley Road and Renton Mine Road. The streets of Avalon have many dead ends, so be careful when selecting your route out of town. It may be best to use a phone navigation app to help route you out of town to the trailhead, as there is full cell service in Avalon.

When you first exit the ferry in Avalon, it may seem natural to follow the coastline east along Pebbly Beach Road. On a map, the trailhead is east and, at a glance, it looks like Pebbly Beach Road leads straight to the trailhead. In actuality this road will leave you way below the trailhead with a very steep hill and nasty bushwhack between you and the trail. If you do follow Pebbly Beach Road east, continue 1.1 miles to Wrigley Road and turn right, then follow Wrigley Road 0.6 miles to the trailhead. This is roughly the same distance as walking through town, but you will not have any amenities along Pebbly Beach Road.

The route through town will bring you into the heart of Avalon. From the ferry terminal, head west into the main town center along Pebbly Beach Road. Looking up to the east, you will see Wrigley Road above several terraces of houses and roads. It may be tempting to follow the power lines and shortcut through houses up to Wrigley Road, but the recommended route is to head southwest through town and catch Wrigley Terrace Road (appears as Wridley Road and Wrigley Road on some maps), which turns into Wrigley Road at its intersection with Clemente Avenue. Follow Wrigley Road 1.2 miles to the trailhead at Renton Mine Road.

Alternatively, you could shortcut almost 5 miles out of the eastern portion of the TCT by heading 1.7 miles up to the Hermit Gulch Campground along Avalon Canyon Road. From Hermit Gulch Campground either continue 1.7 up the Hermit Gulch Trail to the TCT at Divide Road or 0.3 miles up Avalon Canyon Road to the Wrigley Botanical Garden ($7 admission for adults), then another 1.2 miles up to the TCT at Divide Road 0.8 miles south of the Hermit Gulch Trail junction.

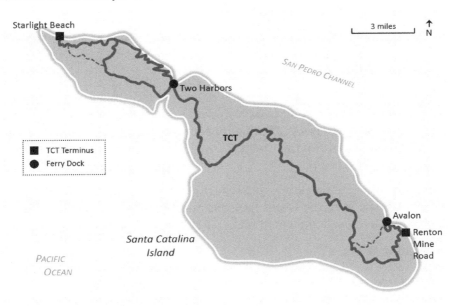

Figure 4 – Main TCT Access Points and Terminuses

Below is a summary of the options from the Avalon ferry terminal:

- 1.8 miles from ferry to TCT trailhead at Wrigley Rd, then 6.4 miles to Hermit Gulch/Divide Road TCT junction = 8.2 miles

- 1.7 miles from ferry to Hermit Gulch Campground, then 1.7 miles to Hermit Gulch/Divide Road TCT junction = 3.4 miles

- 1.7 miles from ferry to Hermit Gulch Campground, then 0.26 miles to Wrigley Botanical Garden, then 1.4 miles to Divide Road, then 0.8 miles to Hermit Gulch/Divide Road TCT junction = 4.2 miles

There are trolley and taxi services available to the Wrigley Road Trailhead, Hermit Gulch Campground, and Wrigley Botanical Garden via Catalina Transportation Services (+1 (310) 510-0025). The simplest solution is to walk to the trailhead. It is an easy section and you get great views of Avalon Bay.

Trail Sections

If your schedule will not allow you to hike the full length of the island, you can tackle a smaller section and use some of the island transportation services to facilitate your section hike.

- Avalon to Two Harbors (without hiking the west end of the island): 28.1 miles and would leave you conveniently at a ferry terminal on either end of your hike.

- Western Loop via Silver Peak: 20.3 miles. 12.8 miles from Two Harbors to Parsons' Landing (over Silver Peak, then down the west end of Silver Peak to Starlight Beach), taking you through the most remote areas of the island. 7.5 miles from Parsons' Landing back to Two Harbors.

A variety of section hikes is possible from various starting and ending points, using one of the island transportation services listed above. Check the schedules closely though to make sure they work with your ferry times.

Navigation & Maps

The TCT is very well-marked with clear, large trail signs at almost every turn along the way. There are also mile markers along the route. Use these to track progress and confirm you are still on the trail. Even though the TCT is well-marked, it is extremely important to be aware of your surroundings and able to read your map in case you find yourself off the route and following one of the many side trails and roads on the island. The mile markers can confirm you are on track if you are ever unsure. But they are spaced a mile apart, so there may not always be one nearby when you need it.

The trail is easy to follow because most of the route is along wide fire roads. Occasionally, the route will follow a single-track trail, so pay close attention to signage if a single-track trail breaks from a fire road. This route could easily be followed with just a map. You should always have a compass with you in case you get particularly confused at some point, but you likely will not need it much. A GPS device is not necessary.

Figure 5 – TCT Trail Signage

Maps are available from the Catalina Island Conservancy website (*http://www.catalinaconservancy.org*) for free or you can pick up a hard copy for $3 at the Conservancy House in Avalon (125 Clarissa Ave). In addition, there are maps for specific areas like the east end of the island, Blackjack and the Airport in the Sky, Little Harbor, and the west end around Silver Peak. These are also available from the Conservancy's website and show a little more detail than the full island map.

I have created a map set using CalTopo that shows the route as well as points of interest along the way. It is not based on a GPS track but shows the routing accurately. You can view the map online and print your own maps from the site. I recommend using the MapBuilder Topo layer when printing, but keep in mind that mileages displayed may not be relevant to the TCT, and some side trails shown could be unmaintained.

Link to custom TCT CalTopo map: *http://caltopo.com/m/G9ES*

(Click 'Export' in the top left corner of the screen for options to download GPS data.)

Trail Regulations

There aren't any exceptional regulations for hiking the TCT. Simply do not disturb or remove any wildlife, rocks, or artifacts along the trail. There is no camping or fires allowed outside of designated areas. Dogs are permitted on the TCT and at all Catalina Island Conservancy campgrounds, but not at Catalina Island Company campgrounds (Hermit Gulch and Two Harbors). Dogs must be on a leash to avoid disturbing wildlife.

Sections of the TCT are open to bicyclists. It is possible to bike from Avalon to Parsons' Landing using alternate routes for sections of the TCT where bikes are not permitted. A bike pass is required and only available by becoming a member of the Catalina Island Conservancy for $35. Visit the Catalina Island Conservancy website for more information on biking the TCT.

Future Trail Alignment

As of the publishing of this book, the Catalina Island Conservancy is undergoing a trails expansion program called *Trekking Catalina.* This program will rehab existing and unofficial trails to create access to different highlights around the island through hiker-friendly and environmentally sound trail construction. There are three segments of the TCT that could be affected by this program. None will significantly alter mileage or routing and most likely will make the grade easier, single-track, and improve signage. These three segments are further described in Appendix G.

b. Points of Interest

As the TCT travels across Santa Catalina Island, there are many areas to explore off the trail and gain a more complete experience of the natural and human history of the mountains. The following list includes a few suggested locations in order from east to west.

Wrigley Casino: Iconic building on the harbor in Avalon. Completed in 1929, it no longer hosts gambling but houses a museum, ballroom, and movie theatre, which are open to the public.

Descanso Beach Club: Private beach club in Avalon with bar and restaurant. Open to the public. Base camp for activities like zip-lining, climbing walls, and kayaking. They host beach parties and the world-famous Catalina Wine Mixer in the summer.

Mt. Ada: Original Wrigley home on the island, named for Ada Wrigley, William Wrigley Jr.'s wife. You pass right by it on the walk from Avalon to the eastern terminus. Currently, it's a bed and breakfast but open to the public for lunch.

Nature Center at Avalon Canyon: On the way to Hermit Gulch Campground and the Wrigley Botanical Garden lies the Nature Center at Avalon Canyon. Stop in for exhibits on the natural history and conservation of Catalina Island. Free admission. Open 7 days a week, 10:00 AM to 4:00 PM.

Wrigley Memorial and Botanic Garden: The botanical garden houses all of Catalina's endemic plant species as well as a variety of other rare cacti, trees, and shrubs from around the world. The memorial building was completed in 1934 in honor of William Wrigley Jr. and uses materials from Catalina Island for most of the prominent  features. Easily accessible from Avalon, the entrance gate is 0.26 miles west of Hermit Gulch Campground. You can access the TCT by continuing 1.4 miles from the entrance gate along the Wrigley Memorial Trail and connect with the TCT 0.8 miles east of the Hermit Gulch Summit shade structure. Admission is $7 or free for members of the Catalina Island Conservancy.

Mount Orizaba (2,097 ft.): The high point of Catalina Island and only 1.4 miles from Blackjack Campground. Unfortunately, the summit is graded, fenced, and home to radio antennae. There are still excellent views of the entire island [pictured on next page], so you can look out at the landscape you will be traversing over the next few days to complete the TCT. There are two gates you need to cross to reach the summit. This is allowed as long as you don't interfere with any property on the mountain. The first fence is for control of the bison population and the second is for the communications area. Cross the first fence and continue up to the second one for views but don't interfere with the communications equipment. Take the opportunity to hike to the top and truly conquer the island from top to bottom.

Blackjack Mountain (2,010 ft.): Second-highest point on the island and only 1.2 miles from Blackjack Campground. The true summit is gated and covered in communication towers, but you can still take in the views of the island near the top.

Ironwood Groves: Visit these rare endemic species in their natural habitat. From Blackjack Campground, head north on the TCT, then continue east on the Cape Canyon Trail 1.3 miles to Airport Road. Head north on Airport Road 200 feet and turn right onto the less-traveled Echo Lake Road for 0.2 miles. The ironwood groves will be to the east down a separate trail. They are shown on the Catalina Island Conservancy's map of the airport area.

El Rancho Escondido: Formerly owned by the Wrigley family, now a vineyard that will open to the public in the next few years. Visible to the south from Sheep Chute Road near Little Harbor.

Banning House Lodge: Built in 1910 and the home of the Banning brothers, who sold Catalina Island to William Wrigley Jr., it is now a bed and breakfast. You pass it on your left as you hike into Two Harbors from Avalon.

Civil War Barracks: Now occupied by the Isthmus Yacht Club in Two Harbors, this building housed Union soldiers during the Civil War, who were evaluating Santa Catalina Island as an internment camp for Native Americans.

Mount Torquemada (1,336 ft.): Offers views of Two Harbors from a dramatic cliff over the coastline. When you reach Water Tank Rd on the climb up to Silver Peak, continue 200 feet uphill on the TCT, then head west 0.7 miles off the TCT on a use trail to the summit.

Silver Peak (1,804 ft.): One of the more secluded summits on the island and the high point on its west end [pictured below]. Continue 1 mile west on the Silver Peak Trail when the TCT turns north and begins its steep descent to Parsons' Landing. You can continue 1.7 miles from the summit down the west end of Silver Peak and reconnect with the TCT 1 mile from Starlight Beach.

West Peak (673 ft.): Even more secluded than Silver Peak but not as high. Take in views of the western edge of the island not visible from Starlight Beach. The route is cross country with a faint use trail through prickly pear cacti and rocky ridgelines. Avoid disturbing the environment by walking on durable surfaces and observe any wildlife, particularly nesting birds, from a distance. Turn west off the TCT 0.6 miles from Starlight Beach onto a brief portion of dirt road to gain the main ridge. Follow the use trail 0.6 miles to the summit of West Peak.

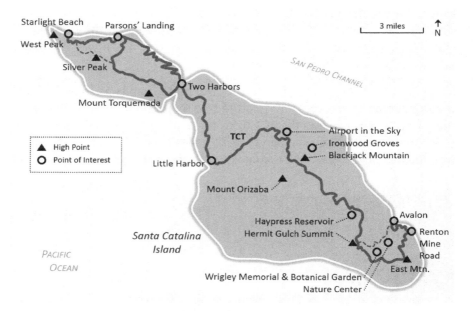

Figure 6 – Points of Interest along the TCT

c. Weather

Southern California's weather is typified by mild winters and hot summers with very little rainfall annually and almost virtually no precipitation in the summer. Consequently, summer is not recommended for hiking due to the sun exposure along the TCT and potentially high temperatures unless you have experience backpacking under those conditions. Your best opportunity for wildflowers is in the spring. Snow and freezing temperatures are extremely rare.

April is recommended for peak conditions considering temperatures, rainfall potential, and wildflowers. October through May would be the best time to avoid summer heat, although there is some chance you will experience rain, so check the forecast for storms and pack accordingly.

Temperature and Precipitation

The chart on the next page shows average monthly high and low temperatures as well as precipitation for the Catalina Airport.

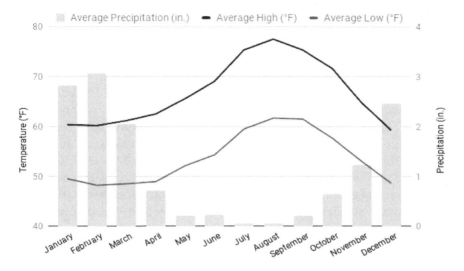

Source: National Oceanic & Atmospheric Administration's monthly climate normals data.

Figure 7 – Average Temperatures and Precipitation (Catalina Airport)

d. Camping

The following section includes all pertinent information for planning your campsites along the TCT, including distances, elevations, amenities, and booking information. Any campsite that could potentially be used while hiking the TCT is included. Other camping options on Catalina Island, such as boat-in camping, that are not likely to be used off the TCT are not included.

Regulations

Camping regulations on Catalina Island are what you would expect of a typical campground. Keep your campsite clean, respect your neighbors, and follow the current fire restrictions. There is no camping allowed outside of established campgrounds. Pets are not allowed at Hermit Gulch and Two Harbors campgrounds.

Permit

There is no physical camping permit required, although the Catalina Island Conservancy asks that you check-in to your campsite by calling the Two Harbors Visitor Services in Two Harbors at +1 (310) 510-4205. If you are starting at Two Harbors, stop in and they will give you a physical permit (open at 8:00 AM), but it is not necessary if you are starting from Avalon.

Campfire

Campfires are permitted in established fire pits, although this is extremely variable and subject to change depending on drought conditions. There is no harvesting of wood allowed anywhere on the island, so if you plan on enjoying a campfire, arrange to have firewood delivered to your site by calling Two Harbors Visitor Services in Two Harbors when you check in for camping. Confirm that your campground allows fires as those regulations change depending on conditions. Check with the Catalina Island Conservancy Ranger Office if you are not sure by calling +1 (310) 510-0393. Currently, there are no fires allowed at Blackjack or Hermit Gulch Campgrounds, but they are allowed at Parsons' Landing, Little Harbor, and Two Harbors. You can purchase special Duraflame® logs at the Hermit Gulch campground store, which meet Avalon fire code requirements, to have a fire at Hermit Gulch Campground.

On-site Rangers

There will be rangers living on site at Two Harbors and Little Harbor during the busy summer months. The rest of the year, rangers will patrol the various campgrounds throughout the day but not be available on-site 24/7. Hermit Gulch Campground has a staffed campground office with camping supplies available for purchase.

Food Storage

There are no restrictions on food storage, although it is highly recommended to protect your food from foxes and squirrels by hanging it, using an animal proof container, or by using a locker at one of the campgrounds. Usually, there are unlocked lockers for food storage available without purchasing a locker in advance. No lockers are available at Little Harbor. The endemic squirrel and fox species on Catalina Island have a reputation for being aggressive towards hiker food bags.

Established Campsites

There are five established campsites along the TCT. They range from potentially crowded camping near the population centers of Two Harbors and Avalon to secluded beach camping at Parsons' Landing and Little Harbor. The campsites must be reserved in advance through *ReserveAmerica.com* (up to one year prior to your arrival date). It is highly recommended that you check availability once you have a date in mind for your trip. Depending on the season, some of the campgrounds can fill up with large groups.

All camping reservations are made through *ReserveAmerica.com* or by calling +1 (877) 478-1487. Search "Catalina" on the *ReserveAmerica.com* website and the list of Catalina's campgrounds will show up. Whether you call or book online, a $9.25 reservation fee will be added for each campsite you book. If you book for multiple people or multiple nights at one campground, only one $9.25 fee will be applied, unless your group is large enough to require multiple sites at the same campground. Rates vary depending on the season and are a few dollars more in the summer (March through October) than in the winter.

The online booking system may tell you that there are two- or three-night minimum stays required for these campgrounds. In these cases, call the Two Harbors Visitor Services at +1 (310) 510-4205 or email *social@scico.com.* Inform them that you are a TCT hiker, and they can spread the two nights over different campgrounds to meet this requirement. All campsites have running water (except for Parsons' Landing), picnic tables, restrooms, fire pits, and trash cans.

Listed from east to west, the five campsites are:

Hermit Gulch

Location:	1.7 miles from the ferry terminal in Avalon
Details:	Lighted bathroom with flush toilets, sink with soap, vending machine, and a microwave. Quarter-operated showers (no hot water, $0.25/minute, change available from staff at camp store) and lockers ($1.25), but lockers are free for food storage. No wood fires allowed, but Duraflame® logs are permitted and available at the camp store. Charcoal is allowed in the standing grills at each campsite and also available at the camp store. Camp store/office and rental equipment on-site (closes at 9:00 PM). Camping fee: $24/night (summer) or $22/night (winter), plus $9.25 reservation fee. You can make last minute payments at the campground. This is the closest campground to Avalon, so it is likely to fill up during the summer and potentially any weekend throughout the year. 6-person tent cabins available for an additional $60/night. Access to the Nature Center, Hermit Gulch Summit, Wrigley Memorial and Botanical Garden.

Blackjack Campground

Location:	15.7 miles from ferry terminal in Avalon via TCT
Details:	Outdoor shower and lockers for food storage. Camping fee: $17/night, plus $9.25 reservation fee. High likelihood of a Catalina fox going for your food bag. If there are free lockers available, store your food in them. Access to Mt. Orizaba, Blackjack Mountain, and Ironwood Groves.

Figure 8 – Hermit Gulch Campground | Little Harbor Campground

Little Harbor

Location:	22.9 miles west of Avalon and 5.2 miles east of Two Harbors
Details:	Outdoor shower, shade structures, and grills. Dogs allowed on leash. Camping fee: $22/night (summer) or $17/night (winter), plus $9.25 reservation fee. Kayak rentals available in advance from Wet Spot Rentals (www.catalinakayaks.com, +1 (310) 510-2229). Fishing allowed with California Fishing License with Ocean Stamp. Two Harbors General Store will deliver gear, groceries, or firewood. Call Two Harbors Visitor Center at +1 (310) 510-4205. Shark Harbor is just south of Little Harbor and there are a few sites on the beach with water, restrooms, picnic tables, and trash cans but no shade. (Select the Shark Harbor sites through the Little Harbor ReserveAmerica.com reservation page.)

[i] Little Harbor Campground sits in a wide, beautiful harbor with plenty of beaches and a dramatic cliff in the middle of the harbor. It is one of the more scenic settings you can camp in, anywhere. If it fits with your hiking schedule, try and stay a night here.

Two Harbors

Location:	0.4 miles east of town
Details:	Shower, shade structures, grills, and equipment rental available on-site. Camping fee: $24/night (summer) or $22/night (winter), plus $9.25 reservation fee. This is very close to Two Harbors, so it is likely to fill up during the summer and potentially any weekend throughout the year. 6-person tent cabins available for an additional $50/night.

Parsons' Landing

Location:	6.6 miles west of Two Harbors via TCT, 4.6 miles east of Starlight Beach and the end of the TCT. Also accessible from Two Harbors via West End Road (7.5 miles).
Details:	This campsite has no water! Reserve a water delivery ($20) with your camping reservation and pick up your locker key at Two Harbors Visitor Services at the foot of the Two Harbors ferry dock. The 2.5-gallon (9.5 liters) water container is left in a locker at the campground along with a bundle of firewood and firestarter log. Camping fee: $22/night (summer) or $17/night (winter), plus $9.25 reservation fee. This is the smallest campground on the TCT with only 8 sites. It is not as popular as the other campgrounds, because it is so secluded. But it can fill up due to a limited number of sites.

[i] If you are hiking the full length of the TCT, you likely will need to stay a night or two at Parsons' Landing, which is great because you get to experience camping on the sand of an isolated beach.

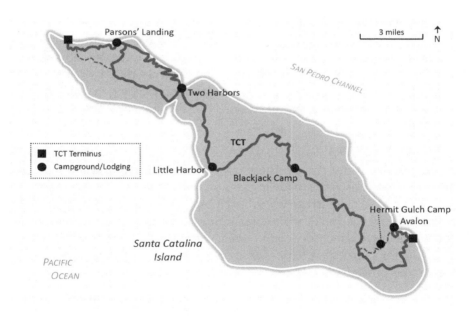

Figure 9 – Campground Locations along the TCT

The table below lists all campgrounds on the TCT along with their cumulative miles from the ferry terminal in Avalon.

Campground	Distance (mi)	Cumulative (mi)	Elevation (ft)
Hermit Gulch	1.7*	1.7*	262
Blackjack	15.7	15.7	1,512
Little Harbor	7.2	22.9	33
Two Harbors (0.4 mi E)	5.2	28.1	39
Parsons' Landing	6.6	34.7	13

* Via Hermit Gulch Trail alternate out of Avalon

Table 4 – Distances between Campgrounds on the TCT

e. Water

Do not expect to find water from a natural source along the trail. Water is only reliably available from established campgrounds and facilities. Take advantage of the potable water provided at these locations and assume that it will be the only water available to you until you reach the next site. Also, do not plan on getting water from the reservoirs throughout the island. These reservoirs are off limits, and they are often fenced and dry. The Haypress Reservoir has piped water in the picnic area right next to the large grill set up. Plan to start the hike with your pack filled to capacity with water, especially coming out of Avalon. The hike to Haypress Reservoir is 10.5 miles.

The good thing about water along the TCT is that, since it is always from a piped, potable water source, there is virtually no situation where you will need to treat your water, allowing you to save weight on water treatment gear. There is no need to carry anything more than water treatment drops in case of emergency and even that might be overkill. In any water emergency, you will be more concerned with finding water than how to treat it. Almost all the water sources are 5 miles apart or greater, with the exception being the 2 miles between Blackjack Campground and the airport.

Plan on carrying and drinking a lot of water to stay hydrated through the steep, sun-exposed climbs on the TCT. A rough rule of thumb for how much water to carry between sources is one liter (about one quart or 34 fl. oz.) per 2-3 miles. If your pack is light and you are comfortable with miles, maybe you can bump that up to 5 miles per liter, but start out conservative and adjust as you progress along the route. Make note of how much water you have left over when you get to the next source. The goal is to carry only a little bit more water than you need. Water, weighing 2.2 pounds per liter, can be the heaviest item in your pack at times. It is obviously lifesaving and essential, but carrying too much can wear you out. Don't just carry the water, drink it while hiking. Get the weight off your back and stay hydrated. Drink lots of water at each water source to ensure you are hydrated before heading out to the next source. The most I carried on the TCT was 3.5 liters, but 5 liters of capacity is recommended depending on your pace and itinerary.

The table below lists all reliable water sources on the TCT, along with their cumulative miles from the ferry terminal in Avalon and distance to the next water source. All sources are potable. There are no reliable natural sources on the TCT.

Water Source	Distance (mi)	Cumulative (mi)	Elevation (ft)
Hermit Gulch Campground	1.7*	1.7*	262
Haypress Reservoir via Hermit Gulch	4.0*	5.7*	1,319
Haypress Reservoir via TCT	10.5	10.5	1,319
Blackjack Campground	5.2	15.7	1,512
Airport in the Sky (0.1 mi N)	2.0	17.7	1,555
Little Harbor	5.2	22.9	33
Two Harbors	5.2	28.1	39
Parsons' Landing via TCT	6.6	34.7	13
Parsons' Landing via Silver Peak	12.8**	40.9**	13
Parsons' Landing to Starlight Beach via TCT (include return)	9.2	43.9	13
Two Harbors via West End Rd	7.5	51.4	39

*Via Hermit Gulch Trail alternate out of Avalon
** Via route over Silver Peak to Starlight Beach

Table 5 – Distances between Water Sources on the TCT

f. Flora & Fauna

The isolated ecosystem of Catalina Island has fostered some of the rarest species on the planet. There are at least 61 endemic species and subspecies found on the island, mostly invertebrates. Hiking the TCT brings you to the backyard of these unique plants and animals as well as hundreds of species that can also be found on the mainland. There are efforts to promote and protect these species on the island while also mitigating competition from non-native species. If you are interested in learning more, there are several books and online resources that will provide more information.

Recommendations for additional reading are provided in the *Links & References* section of the appendix.

Vegetation

Catalina Island contains species typical of chaparral and coastal sage scrub plant communities, including sagebrush, manzanita, island scrub oak, and many types of wildflowers. Native plant species are drought-resistant, subject to occasional wildfire, and can be found throughout similar Mediterranean climates on the mainland. However, some unique variations to the mainland plant communities have been created due to the island's limited gene pool and isolation from mainland species.

There are eight endemic plant species that are only found on Catalina Island, sometimes existing in a single location on the island, and twenty-six island endemic species that are only found on two or more of California's offshore islands. Visit the Wrigley Memorial Garden just outside of Avalon near Hermit Gulch Campground for an introduction to some of these species before encountering them along the TCT in their natural habitat. Plan your hike for February through May for the best chance to catch wildflowers.

Endemic Species

- **Catalina ironwood.** Once found across North America, it is now confined to a few groves on Catalina Island. Several groves exist close to Blackjack Campground. A map of the Blackjack Campground and airport area is available from the Catalina Island Conservancy website and shows the ironwood groves to the east of Blackjack Campground along Airport Road.

Figure 10 – Catalina Ironwood Leaves | Catalina Liveforever

- **Catalina liveforever.** Perennial succulent.

- **Catalina Island mountain mahogany.** Grows wild in a single protected drainage on the island's south side. Your best, and possibly only, opportunity to view this rare shrub is at the Wrigley Botanical Garden.

- **Santa Catalina Island bedstraw.** Flowering shrub.

- **Santa Catalina Island bush-mallow.** Flowering plant with a pink bloom.

- **Santa Catalina Island manzanita.** Species of manzanita with a white bloom.

- **Trask's yerba santa.** Flowering shrub.

- **St. Catherine's lace.** Large ornamental buckwheat with a white bloom.

Non-Endemic Species

- **Prickly pear.** One of several edible plants, along with Miner's lettuce, wild hyacinth, Catalina cherry, bladderpods, and fennel (invasive), found on the island. You will see a lot of prickly pear cacti throughout your hike.

- **Wildflowers** include shooting star, island bush poppy, Indian paintbrush, Catalina mariposa lily, bush sunflowers, giant coreopsis, wild hyacinth, sticky monkey flower, heart-leaved penstemon, and silver bush lupine.

Figure 11 – Prickly Pear | Wildflowers

- **Coastal sage.** Common and fragrant plants brewed into tea by natives of Catalina.

- **Poison oak.** Prevalent throughout the island and will cause severe rash and irritation if contacted. Be very familiar with poison oak's appearance and understand that it can vary greatly from red to green color, from a shiny to dry leaf, and from a vine to a shrub. Follow the "leaves of three, let it be" rule if ever in doubt.

- **Stinging nettle.** Found in stream beds and damp areas. The hairs on the plant cause a painful burning sensation and rash on the skin. The irritation is only temporary and not nearly as severe as poison oak. Stay on the trail to avoid stinging nettle.

Wildlife

Catalina Island was never connected by land to the mainland, so any animal species present had to brave the open ocean to reach Catalina or be introduced by humans, as the bison on Catalina Island famously were. Early arrivals to the island evolved separate from their mainland brethren due to differences in available food sources and predators, resulting in over 53 endemic animal species and subspecies on the island. In some cases, such as the Catalina Island fox, the island variant became smaller than its mainland cousin, the gray fox, while other subspecies, such as the Catalina California quail and Catalina California ground squirrel, are larger than their mainland counterparts.

Endemic Mammals and Birds

- **Santa Catalina Island fox.** The largest endemic mammal and terrestrial predator on the island. They are only found on Catalina Island although five other island gray fox subspecies can be found throughout the Channel Islands. It is thought that Catalina natives brought the fox over from the other Channel Islands thousands of years ago. The Catalina Island fox was almost lost to an outbreak of distemper virus in 1999, which caused the island's fox population to drop from an estimated 1,300 to 100 foxes. Thanks to conservation efforts, the Catalina Island Conservancy estimates there are over 1,800 foxes on the island as of 2015.

- **Santa Catalina Island deer mouse, harvest mouse, shrew, and Hutton's vireo** all appear very similar to their ancestors but are genetically distinct enough to be considered their own subspecies.

- **Catalina California ground squirrel and Catalina California quail** are larger relatives to the California ground squirrel and quail.

Figure 12 – Catalina Ground Squirrel | Catalina Quail (female)

- **Catalina Bewick's wren** is a subspecies of the more common Bewick's wren.

Endemic Invertebrate

- Catalina Island is home to 45 endemic species and subspecies of invertebrates, including the Catalina crab spider, Catalina walkingstick, Catalina shieldback katydid, Jerusalem cricket, painted tiger moth, Catalina orangetip butterfly, and the Avalon hairstreak, which possibly has a smaller habitat range than any insect on earth.

Common Non-Endemic Animals

- **American bison.** Possibly one of the most unusual experiences on the TCT will be running into a herd of bison. No, these guys did not swim across the ocean channel hundreds of years ago. Bison are not native to Southern California. Instead, the bison were brought to the island in 1924 for a few scenes in the ironically named silent film, *The Vanishing American*. The original 14 bison did not make the final cut for the film but were presumably compensated as background actors for their time. When the filming was done, the bison were left on the island to fend for themselves. Over time, more bison were added from the mainland and eventually the herd swelled to several hundred before a sterilization program was put in place. Today, there are roughly 200 bison on the island, and the population is managed by the Catalina Island Conservancy.

Figure 13 – American Bison

- **Southern Pacific rattlesnake.** Only venomous snake on the island.

- **Mule deer.** Non-native species that is having a devastating effect on the island's plant populations, which do not possess natural defenses to large herbivores.

- **Three types of hummingbird.** The Channel Island Allen's hummingbird, migratory Allen's hummingbird, and Anna's hummingbird. The migratory Allen's has a shorter wing, tail, and bill than the Channel Island Allen's hummingbird. Additionally, the Allen's hummingbird is more common than the Anna's hummingbird on Catalina, while the Anna's is more common on the mainland.

- **Dusky or sordida Orange-crowned warbler.** Subspecies of the Orange-crowned warbler endemic to the Channel Islands. Migrates to Baja California for winter.

- **Island loggerhead shrike.** Subspecies endemic to the Channel Islands.

- **Bald eagle.** Several bald eagle pairs nest on Catalina Island. Do not disturb nesting birds if you encounter any.

- **Red-tailed hawk.** Common hawk seen soaring through the sky with a white underside covered in reddish-brown spots.

- **American kestrel.** Look for these raptors perched above Catalina's fields and meadows.

- **Osprey.** Black and white raptor found near water. Dark stripe through its eye and a white underside differentiate it from the bald eagle.

- **Acorn woodpecker.** Common throughout the island. Mostly black body with white underside and spot on the back with red and yellow accent. They store acorns in the trunks of trees. If you see a tree trunk full of holes and acorns, that is the work of acorn woodpeckers.

- **Western meadowlark.** Distinctive yellow breast with black "V". They occupy meadows and have a dreamy, melodic, flute-sounding call.

Figure 14 – Acorn Woodpecker | Western Meadowlark

Although you would have to be extremely lucky, keep an eye to the San Pedro Channel for whale spouts. Blue, fin, minke, and humpback whales pass through as part of their migration to breeding and spawning grounds. There are charter boats available for fishing or to view flying fish just off the coast of the island.

g. Safety

The TCT does not have many high-risk situations that one might encounter along the route. However, it does not hurt to be aware of all possible scenarios. Some safety issues include the following:

Travel along the TCT is very safe. There aren't many people that travel beyond the populated areas of the island and there are few companies licensed to travel on the roads through the island interior. Anyone traveling outside of Avalon is most likely with a guided touring operation and not out on their own looking for trouble. Most people will be tourists checking out the beauty of the island. The campgrounds should feel very safe. Someone would have to go through a lot of trouble to get to these places. Hermit Gulch and Two Harbors campgrounds are closest to population centers. There, you would be most likely to share a campground with rowdy campers.

If you get lost, you are always a day's walk from a population center, usually only a few hours' walk. Cell service is available on a surprising amount of the island as well. It is unlikely you will get lost to a point where you will be in danger. The Blackjack Campground does have trees over some of the campsites, so check for dead tree limbs overhead when selecting a tent site. Several wild animals and plants pose a risk on the island. Be respectful and alert in their presence.

The greatest wildlife risk may be the wild bison. They are very large (although smaller than mainland bison due to their diet) and, if aggravated or feel threatened, could cause serious injury or death. They may look heavy and cumbersome but can run three times the speed of a human. Observe bison from a safe distance. Do not touch, feed, or even approach the bison. If you encounter one blocking the trail, back away and wait for the bison to move off the trail or select an alternate route. Put large objects, like trees and rocks, between you and the bison. Do not surround or surprise a bison.

Catalina fox are the largest land predator on the island, but with adult males only weighing between four and six pounds, they pose a greater risk to your food bag. Ticks have been found on the island and can of course transmit Lyme disease. Check yourself at the end of the day, especially if you have walked through tall grass or overgrown trail. Ticks are best removed by pulling at the head of the tick, closest to the skin, with tweezers. A tick will release its bite if you place the hot end of a recently extinguished match on its back. If the tick is simply crawling on you and has not bit yet, you should be able to just brush them off without risk of Lyme disease.

Figure 15 – Wildlife Warning Signs

Rattlesnakes are also present on the island. They are present year-round but more common in the summer months. Keep aware of your footing while hiking and give plenty of distance if you see a rattlesnake. Pass by the snake at a distance well outside of its striking range, which is roughly two-thirds of its body length. If you are bitten, do not try to cut out or remove the venom. Instead, seek medical help immediately and get to an emergency room as quickly and calmly as possible. If possible, try to avoid any exertion by the victim, as it will circulate the venom in their bloodstream faster.

Poison oak can be found throughout the island. Make sure you are familiar with the its appearance. Follow the "leaves of three, let it be" rule if you encounter any plant on the trail that you are unsure about. The leaves can vary in size and color from green to red to brown depending on the season and condition of the plant. It may appear shiny or dry. Don't assume something is not poison oak, unless you are absolutely sure. Stay alert in the canyons and creek beds, where it is most common. The higher, exposed areas are less likely to have poison oak. Off-trail travel increases your risk of exposure. If you come in contact with poison oak, wash the affected area as soon as possible, preferably with soap if it is available. Try to remove the oils from your skin and clothes. Any clothing that may have come in contact with poison oak should be removed and kept isolated, until it can be washed thoroughly. Poison oak can take one to six days from exposure to show signs of a reaction, but they usually appear within 24 to 48 hours of exposure.

Several stretches of the TCT follow roads, either paved roads in Avalon or dirt roads in the more remote areas of the islands. Vehicle traffic is restricted in the island's interior to a few permitted organizations. Many of the more solitary moments on the TCT occur on these dirt roads. However, you may be passed by eco tours or water tankers and service vehicles for the water systems while walking roads on the east side of the island. These roads also act as access points and fire breaks for wildfire suppression. Stay alert for large-vehicle traffic in these areas.

Sun exposure is constant for many sections of the TCT. Be prepared with proper clothing and seek shade off the trail if you feel the heat getting to you. If the heat and sun is particularly bad, plan on taking extended breaks, naps, and lunch during the hottest portion of the day, typically the early afternoon. The most comfortable times of day to hike may be very early in the morning and at dusk. These also happen to be the best times for wildlife viewing, photography, and solitude. Look ahead for any long sections of climbing and try to avoid hiking those in the early afternoon.

The TCT goes through several well-travelled areas along its route, some with cell phone service. But there are solitary sections of the trail, where you may not see another person for miles. Satellite communicators would add an extra level of safety. However, they are not essential. Always share your itinerary with a third party and update them with your location when possible. Emergency phones are available at Airport in the Sky, Little Harbor, Two Harbors, and Middle Ranch (off the TCT).

In the case of emergency, always call 911. Cell service may not always be available, so, if possible, send one person for help while at least one person remains with the victim. Getting to the population centers of Avalon and Two Harbors, or even the airport or campgrounds, will increase your chances of encountering someone who can call for help or reach cell phone service. The Catalina Island Medical Center is located at 100 Falls Canyon Road, Avalon, CA 90704. Phone number: +1 (310) 510-0700.

h. Other Conditions

Generally, the weather on Catalina Island is stable and pleasant. However, it can experience some extreme environmental and meteorological conditions. The island has been under a drought for several years, making it more susceptible to wildfires and landslides. Almost all of the TCT is on land owned and managed by the Catalina Island Conservancy. Contact the conservancy before heading out for information on closures and conditions. Phone number: +1 (310) 510-2595.

3. What to Expect – Backbone Trail

The Backbone Trail takes you along the spine of the Santa Monica Mountains, among sandstone and volcanic rock formations, and immerses you into the rare Mediterranean climate found only in four other places on earth (the land surrounding the Mediterranean Sea and the coastal areas of Central Chile, South Africa, and Southern Australia). Views of the Pacific Ocean, Channel Islands, inland mountain ranges, and the Los Angeles Basin keep your eyes fixed outward while wildflowers, fossils, and various plant communities occupy your senses on the ground. The combination of climate, topography, and diverse biology make the Santa Monica Mountains a one-of-a-kind destination and a unique backpacking opportunity.

Campsites and water sources are scarce, making thru-hiking a challenge but by no means impossible. The following section presents the information necessary to plan your own thru-hike of the Backbone Trail.

a. Trails & Navigation

The vision of a route through the Santa Monica Mountains has been around for decades. The route came together piece by piece as park lands were established and private land was acquired. But it wasn't until June 4, 2016, that the trail was officially opened as a continuous east-to-west route. The trail systems surrounding the Backbone Trail have been used for a long time by many people, but the complete route is relatively new as of the writing of this book. You may be among the first to hike its length.

The BBT runs 66.8 miles along the Santa Monica Mountains between Will Rogers State Historic Park and the Ray Miller Trailhead in Point Mugu State Park. The trail runs in the east-to-west direction and takes you across state, federal, and private lands along its route. The official length of the trail is listed as 67.2 miles, but that number may not be incorporating new routing since the trail's completion.

Hiking Direction

The trail can be hiked in either the westbound or eastbound direction. There are no major differences between the two directions. Hiking westbound, you will progress towards more remote territory and can end your hike at the Pacific Ocean, but transportation may be more difficult from the Ray Miller Trailhead. There does not seem to be a more popular direction to hike the BBT. Your schedule and transportation options at the trailheads may have the biggest influence on the direction of your hike.

Trail Conditions

The BBT is on well-maintained, single-track trail with some dirt roads along the route. The trail is very well designed with climbs and descents occurring on well-graded trails full of switchbacks.

Figure 16 – Exposed, Single-Track Trail | Wooded Trail Section

There are many sun-exposed sections of the trail, which are great for views but tough when you hit a climb at the wrong time of day. Take it slow in those sections and take a break in any available shade. The BBT has many long, shaded sections as well, so enjoy those while you can.

- **Highest point:** Sandstone Peak (3,111 ft.). The high point of the Santa Monica Mountains, while not officially on the BBT, is accessible by a 0.1-mile side trail. Just before the BBT junction with this side trail, the trail crests around 3,000 feet, which is the highest point actually on the BBT.

- **Lowest point:** Ray Miller Trailhead (33 ft.). Continue out to the ocean just beyond the Ray Miller Trailhead to get down to sea level.

- **Biggest elevation change:** The section between Sandstone Peak (3,111 ft.) and Danielson Ranch (300 ft.) changes 2,811 feet in 6.8 miles. Starting 0.9 miles from Danielson Ranch, the trail gains 2,200 feet in 3.7 miles until you reach Boney Mountain, 2.2 miles from Sandstone Peak.

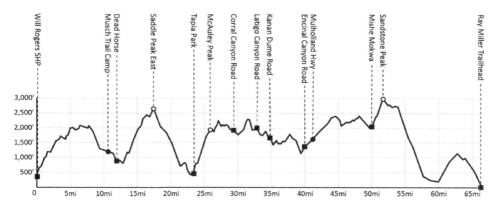

Figure 17 – Elevation Profile of the BBT

Trail Access

There are many roads that intersect the BBT along its route. These access points can facilitate section hikes or travel to off-trail lodging. There is usually cell phone service at these roads if you need to arrange a ride.

The eastern terminus at Will Rogers State Historic Park is only 15 miles, as the crow flies, from downtown Los Angeles. There are many options to get there depending on your origin. The western terminus is another 30 miles west and only accessible from the scenic Pacific Coast Highway (PCH).

Eastern Terminus: Will Rogers State Historic Park (34.0545, -118.5133)

The trailhead is located between the parking lot and tennis courts immediately past the entrance gate. Follow the white railing out of the parking area along the hiking trail with the bikes restricted site.

Parking is available. However, signage will not show overnight parking is available. For overnight parking, visit the ranger station or talk to any park employee. Provide your return date, and they will create a notice to place in your car. Water and restrooms are available. The state park occasionally hosts large events, which may limit parking availability. There is no camping at Will Rogers State Historic Park.

Western Terminus: Ray Miller Trailhead (34.0863, -119.0367)

The trailhead is located on the side of the road entering the parking lot area. There are brown signs at the trailhead.

Parking is available at the western terminus, but the gate will be locked at night around 10:00 PM, meaning your car could be locked in the parking area if you arrive after dark. Signs in the parking lot say the lot closes at "sunset", but the sunset deadline is generous and roughly 10:00 PM. Give yourself an extra hour to be sure in case the employee locking the gate comes a little early that night. Additionally, there is contradicting signage at the parking area that gives the impression overnight parking is not allowed. But it is the primary access point for the La Jolla Valley Walk-in Camp, and the self-service parking meters have options for purchasing overnight parking. Purchase enough days of parking to cover your trip and leave a note on your car stating your return date and that you are hiking the Backbone Trail.

There is camping at the western terminus. Walk out of the parking area to the beach and right across the highway is Thornhill Broome Beach, a perfect place to reflect at the end of a long hike. See Section 3d *Camping* for details.

Intermediary Access Points

The BBT crosses many roads along its route that could be used to facilitate section hikes, take a night off the trail in town, or stage water caches. Parking restrictions and facilities vary from trailhead to trailhead. Hitchhiking may be difficult on some of the roads where traffic will be moving very fast with little shoulder room to pull over. The following figure presents the main BBT trailheads between the eastern and western terminuses.

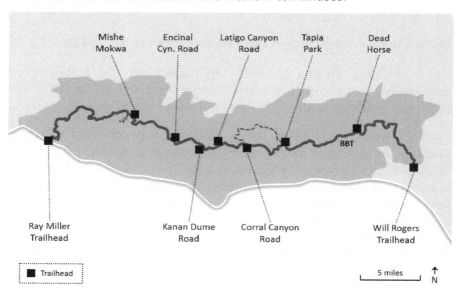

Figure 18 – Main Trailheads along the BBT

The table below lists all road access points along the BBT as well as their cumulative miles from the Will Rogers Trailhead.

Road Access Point	Dist. (mi)	Cumulative (mi)	Elevation (ft)
Eastern Terminus - Will Rogers SHP	0	0	433
Trippet Ranch (0.1 mi S) via Musch Camp	10.8	10.8	1,195
Dead Horse TH at Topanga Canyon Blvd	1.2	12.0	850
Old Topanga Canyon Road	0.7	12.8	774
Stunt Road Overlook	4.1	16.9	2,360
Piuma Road Crossing	4.8	21.7	728
Piuma Rd (WB: W at road, 0.3 mi to Malibu Cyn Rd EB: S at signed trail.)	1.4	23.1	459
Tapia Park TH (Malibu Creek CG 1.9 mi N) at Malibu Canyon Rd	0.5	23.6	490
Corral Canyon Rd Trailhead	5.3	28.9	1,998
Latigo Canyon Rd Trailhead	4.2	33.1	2,037
Kanan Dume Rd/Newton Cyn TH	2.3	35.4	1,529
Zuma Ridge Trail (PCH 6.1 mi S)	2.6	38.0	1,788
Encinal Canyon Rd Trailhead	2.3	40.3	1,401
Mulholland Highway	1.2	41.5	1,621
Yerba Buena Rd	4.4	45.9	2,080
Mishe Mokwa TH (Yerba Buena Rd)	4.6	50.5	2,103
Western Terminus - Ray Miller TH	16.3	66.8	33

Table 6 – Road Access Points along the BBT

Trail Sections

Suggestions for two- or three-day section hikes are listed below. If you want to section-hike the complete length of the BBT, a good intermediate point would be between Malibu Creek State Park and Circle X Ranch to break up the longest stretch of trail without water and campgrounds. There are many side trips off the BBT, which are further described in the *Points of Interest* section below, that could extend the mileage of a section-hike. The Zuma Ridge Trail, at BBT mile 38, heads 5.5 miles south to Malibu and the beach near a bus stop that services Malibu and Santa Monica, which could also be a good intermediary point.

Will Rogers State Historic Park to Latigo Canyon Rd/Kanan Dume Rd (33.1-35.4 miles)

Hike the eastern portion of the trail through Topanga State Park, past Eagle Rock, over Saddle Peak, through Malibu Creek State Park, and over the ridgeline west of Malibu Creek State Park. End your hike at one of the many road crossings west of Malibu Creek State Park, depending on your desired mileage, or take the Zuma Ridge Trail near Kanan Dume Road, described in Sections 3b *Points of Interest* and 4c *Travel Arrangements* below, to access Malibu beaches and bus connections back to Santa Monica and Los Angeles. Camping at Musch Trail Camp and Malibu Creek State Park.

Mishe Mokwa Trailhead to the western terminus at Ray Miller Trailhead (16.3 miles)

This section takes you over Sandstone Peak, past Tri-Peaks, and into the remote western areas of the Santa Monica Mountains. Explore the highlands of the Boney Mountain formation around Sandstone Peak or vast meadows in La Jolla Valley to extend the trip. Spend a night at the most secluded campground on the trail, La Jolla Valley Walk-in Camp. Camping at Circle X Ranch, Danielson Ranch, and La Jolla Valley Walk-in Camp.

Navigation & Maps

One of the difficult aspects of hiking the trail is the lack of clear signage at trail junctions and road crossings. The Santa Monica Mountains contain a huge network of trails that intersect the BBT at many points. There are also many unofficial use trails, which break off to lookouts or shortcut to official trails. These will not be signed and can be confused for the BBT. For this reason, it is important to be aware of your surroundings and use all available information in case you come across an unsigned, or even signed, junction you are not sure about. Two of the most confusing locations are:

- **Topanga Canyon Blvd (Highway 27) and Old Topanga Canyon Road:** Between these two road crossings is an elementary school with its own trail network near the BBT. These trails, in addition to lack of signage, can lead to confusion. WB hikers: After climbing up from Topanga Canyon Blvd (Hwy 27), reach a motorway in 0.3 miles. Head downhill (southeast) on the motorway towards the school, then turn west towards water tanks and pick up the trail on the west end of the water tanks. EB hikers: Follow the water tanks onto a paved path going towards the school. Turn northwest onto motorway for 240 feet, then turn east onto BBT.

- **Stunt Road Overlook:** The BBT crosses right at the crossroads of Saddle Peak Road, Stunt Road, and the Topanga Tower Motorway. WB hikers: Trail splits the fork between Stunt and Saddle Peak Road west of intersection. EB hikers: Approaching the crossroads, stay on the ridge, do not drop down to the north onto Stunt Rd, which will lead to a brief road walk. Immediately east of the overlook and parking area, take the rough paved road past the gate, following the overhead power lines. In less than 0.1 miles turn southeast at BBT sign.

Figure 19 – Sparse BBT Trail Signage

The BBT route occasionally follows older and more well-established trails, such as the Musch Trail, Mishe Mowka Trail, and the Etz Meloy Motorway. In those cases, trail signs may omit reference to the BBT and use the older trail's name. Don't think you are off the route just because you have not seen "Backbone Trail" on any of the recent signs. Know the names of your upcoming destinations and trails to determine the correct trail if "Backbone Trail" is not on any of the signage.

A map and compass are your friends in these situations. When you are confused, the first thing to do is to find your location on a map. Take note of the direction you have been hiking in, any recent changes in direction of the trail, visible or recently passed roads and facilities, the surrounding topography (are you on a hill or in a valley?), and your last known location. Use this information to locate yourself on the map and then assess the correct trail. If you are truly stumped, there is a good chance you may have cell signal to find your location on a smartphone.

[i] In general, follow the more obvious, well-worn trail and ignore most of the unmarked trails that break from the main route. Use these trails occasionally for an improved vantage point above the BBT.

There are two locations in the eastern portion of the trail, within Topanga State Park, where the trail will split and then rejoin with little difference in mileage. One occurs between Eagle Junction and the Hub, where the trail splits north to Eagle Rock or south to Eagle Springs. There is negligible difference in mileage between the two. From Eagle Junction west to Trippet Ranch, you can take either the Musch Trail to the Musch Trail Camp, the only camping in the area, or the East Topanga Fire Road (also called Eagle Springs Fire Road) south to Trippet Ranch, which stays high on an open ridge and is 0.5 miles shorter but does not pass the campground. Mileage reported in this book uses the route to Eagle Rock and along the Musch Trail past the campground.

Maps

A good map set is important for the reasons mentioned above, and I would recommend the National Geographic Trails Illustrated map, number 253 "Santa Monica Mountains National Recreation Area". The map is $12 and available online or at most outdoor retailers in the Los Angeles area. It covers the entire trail in one map, front and back, with enough detail for navigation purposes. The BBT is highlighted yellow on the map. It also covers much of the surrounding area from the ocean to the valley north of the mountains, which is very useful for a big picture look at the area in case you will be accessing the trail from one of the many road intersections or need to get off the trail at some point.

Another great option would be the Tom Harrison map sets, which I did not use for this trail but have used for other trails. They provide a great amount of detail. You would need four maps to cover the trail: Pt. Mugu State Park, Zuma-Trancas Canyon, Malibu Creek State Park, and Topanga State Park. Each map costs $10, and they are available online or at local outdoor retailers. The National Park Service also has a map that does not provide much detail but highlights the facilities and roads along the route. I would not recommend this map for navigation, although it is to scale and shows the route accurately.

Link: *https://www.nps.gov/samo/planyourvisit/upload/BBT-Brochure-2016-web.pdf*

Since the trail has only recently been completed, there will be a few sections shown as private property or closed until these map sets are updated and republished. This should not affect your ability to navigate the route using these maps. Just keep in mind that sections previously marked private are now open and signage will be clear at those locations for the new route.

I have created a map set using CalTopo that shows the updated route as well as points of interest along the way. It is not based on a GPS track but shows the routing accurately. You can view the map online and print your own maps from the site. I recommend using the MapBuilder Topo layer when printing, but keep in mind that mileages displayed may not be relevant to the BBT and some side trails shown could be unmaintained.

Link to custom BBT CalTopo map: *http://caltopo.com/m/D1JH*

GPS

I did not find it necessary to have a GPS for navigation, but if you are not confident with map reading, it may be helpful in the case of unclear intersections with other trails. The NPS has GPS points available for download on their website.

Link: *https://www.nps.gov/samo/planyourvisit/upload/BBT-west-to-east-via-points-2009.pdf*

Keep in mind that these points do not include two recently-opened sections of trail and instead show a road walk around them. Follow the trail instead of the road walk. These two sections are very short, so the GPS points will be good for most of the existing route.

Cell service is available for a lot of the trail. You cannot be sure it will be available when you are lost, but it could be useful in some situations to find your location with a smartphone mapping application.

Trail Regulations

The BBT is a mixed-use trail for some sections. Equestrians and mountain bikers are allowed on some parts of the trail. Always yield to equestrians, step way off the trail and avoid spooking horses while they pass. You are more likely to come across mountain bikers than horses, and you may even see more bikers than other backpackers. Technically, bikers are supposed to yield to hikers but usually there is not a lot of room on the side of the trail for bikes to pull over, so I almost always yield to bikers. It  is much easier and safer for me to take one step to the side of the trail than it is for a biker to kill all their momentum and quickly find a place beside the trail with enough room to stop.

Dogs are not allowed on the backcountry trails of any of the three California State Parks the BBT goes through. This affects a significant portion of the trail including both the eastern terminus in Topanga State Park and the western terminus in Point Mugu State Park. Dogs are allowed at the Malibu Creek State Park campground but not on any trails. Dogs are allowed on National Park Service land, which includes Sandstone Peak, but must be on a leash. There is no camping or fires allowed outside of designated areas.

Equestrians

If you are going to ride the BBT on horseback, there are some important issues to be aware of. Grazing is not allowed, so you must carry all your feed. Also, water sources are very sparse, so you will likely need to carry all your water as well. A good solution is to have people meet you at road crossings and campgrounds with feed and water. Scatter manure among brush away from the camping areas.

Camping restrictions apply at some sites, and you may need to request special permission from the park agencies to camp. Musch Trail Camp has corrals, but you cannot drive up to the campground to deliver supplies. Equestrian camping is not allowed at Malibu Creek State Park, La Jolla Valley Walk-in, Thornhill Broome, and Leo Carrillo State Park campgrounds. Cleft of the Rock Ranch would allow equestrians, but check first to make sure they are available. Circle X Ranch and Danielson Ranch would require special permission from the park agencies, NPS and California SP, respectively.

[i] For more information about riding the BBT, contact Ruth Gerson of the Santa Monica Mountains Trails Council at *ruthgerson@aol.com*. Ruth led the first complete ride of the BBT after its official opening in June, 2016.

b. Points of Interest

As the BBT winds through the Santa Monica Mountains, there are many areas to explore off the trail and gain a more complete experience of the natural and human history of the mountains. The following list includes a few suggested locations in order from east to west.

Will Rogers State Historic Park: Located at the eastern terminus. Will Rogers was a cowboy and one of the biggest stars of the 1930s. His former ranch is now the Will Rogers State Historic Park. You can tour his ranch house, take a horseback ride, or watch a polo game at the only polo field in Los Angeles.

Rustic Canyon and Murphy's Ranch: An alternate out of Will Rogers State Historic Park takes you through rugged Rustic Canyon and past a compound of long-abandoned buildings that, according to local oral history, was home to a community of Nazi sympathizers in the 1930s, called Murphy's Ranch. The compound was raided after the bombing of Pearl Harbor and later became an artist community before falling into disrepair. Currently, the buildings are covered in graffiti art that give you a haunting sense of what life was like in the canyon. A few dilapidated structures were torn down and others boarded up for safety reasons in 2016. The hike through Rustic Canyon is unmaintained but offers an opportunity to start the climb out of Will Rogers State Historic Park in the shade.

Eagle Rock (1,957 ft.): A huge boulder outcrop with panoramic views right off the BBT, 8.4 miles from the eastern terminus at Will Rogers State Historic Park. Traveling westbound from the Hub (mile 7.4), take the northern Eagle Rock Trail rather than the southern Eagle Springs Trail. Eastbound take the Eagle Rock Trail heading uphill when the Musch Trail connects with the East Topanga Fire Road.

Topanga Lookout (2,469 ft.): A viewpoint an easy 0.9-mile hike from the BBT, east of the crossing of Stunt Road.

Saddle Peak East (2,805 ft.): This broad, open summit gives panoramic views of the city of Los Angeles, Santa Monica Bay, and the Pacific Ocean. Saddle Peak West, the high point of the eastern Santa Monica Mountains, sits immediately to the west and is slightly higher but is covered in communications towers. On occasion, the gate is open and access is possible. Access Saddle Peak East by a 0.2-mile side trail 0.7 miles west of the Stunt Road Trailhead at BBT mile 17.6.

Malibu Hindu Temple: Traditional Hindu temple east of Malibu Creek State Park. It is one of the largest in the U.S. Visiting hours are 9:00 AM to noon and 5:00 PM to 8:00 PM weekdays and 8:00 AM to 8:00 PM weekends.

Rock Pools: Popular local watering hole in Malibu Creek State Park. Convenient access if you are camping in the park or taking the Bulldog Motorway from the campground to the BBT. There are signs warning against drinking the water but swimming is fine. This may be your only chance to cool off until you reach the ocean at the Ray Miller Trailhead.

Paramount Ranch: Film location for over 100 TV shows and 200 movies starting in 1927. Access via Yearling Trail or Crags Road to Lake Vista Drive from Malibu Creek State Park, over 2 miles one way. The ranch has an historic 2-mile racetrack that hosted races in the mid-1950s.

M*A*S*H Site: Film location for the TV series in Malibu Creek State Park, 2.5 miles west of the campground. You can continue up Bulldog Motorway 4.5 miles to reconnect with the BBT at Corral Canyon Trailhead.

McAuley Peak (2,049 ft.): A short climb up the summit block gives panoramic views of the ridges and peaks around Malibu Creek State Park. Look for the peak immediately east of the trail, 2.8 miles west of the Tapia Park Trailhead. Named for Milt McAuley, who was instrumental in the planning, promotion, and preservation

of the Backbone Trail, as well as the rest of the Santa Monica Mountain trail systems, through his guidebooks and hiking classes at a time when the mountains were at a crossroads of conservation and development.

Castro Peak (2,827 ft.): Off-limits. The only reason it is mentioned is because the ridgeline to the peak appears on maps that it connects to the BBT from Corral Canyon Trailhead and would make a good side trail. But there is an absurdly armored gate blocking access to the highest peak in the central Santa Monica Mountains.

Peak 1984 (1,984 ft.): Take in sweeping views of Zuma Canyon all the way to the Pacific Ocean from the secluded open summit of Peak 1984. You won't find many other hikers here, as the unmaintained trail can be overgrown, but there is an obvious consistent footpath to the summit. Option to continue down into Zuma Canyon and  then south to the Pacific Ocean in Malibu at Zuma Beach and Point Dume.

Malibu Beach access via Zuma Canyon: Two options exist to access Malibu beaches and the bus servicing Malibu and Santa Monica while staying entirely on the trail before reaching the neighborhoods in Malibu. At the Kanan Dume Road Trailhead, BBT mile 35.4, head up to Peak 1984 and continue into Zuma Canyon (7.6 miles to PCH/Trancas) or take the Zuma Ridge Trail at BBT mile 38 (6.1 miles to PCH/Trancas).

Newton Canyon Falls and Upper Zuma Falls: Seasonal waterfalls between Kanan Dume Road and Encinal Canyon Road. Newton Canyon Falls is west off the BBT at the small Backbone Trail sign, 0.3 miles west of the Kanan Dume Road trailhead. Upper Zuma Falls [pictured to the right] is accessed via a 0.2-mile unmaintained trail that breaks off east from the BBT, 2 miles west of the Kanan Dume Road trailhead.

Sandstone Peak (3,111 ft.): High point of the Santa Monica Mountains and accessible by a 0.1-mile side trail off the BBT with views of Mt. Baldy to the east and the Channel Islands to the west [pictured on next page].

Inspiration Point (2,800 ft.): Outstanding viewpoint among rock formations just south of the BBT, 0.9 miles west of the Sandstone Peak side trail.

Tri-Peaks and Tri-Peaks Caves (3,010 ft.): Rocky summit on the Boney Mountain formation west of Sandstone Peak. Accessible by a 0.5-mile side trail off the BBT. There are two connecting trails from the BBT, which then converge before reaching Tri-Peaks. No matter the direction you are hiking, take the first signed side trail  to Tri-Peaks and, at the first junction, where the two side trails converge, drop packs and then continue north to Tri-Peaks. You can then return to the BBT via the other connecting trail at this junction without having to fully backtrack. Climbing the Tri-Peaks summit block requires class 3 climbing, easiest route is on the north side. A network of caves around the summit is accessible by following the footpath up to the summit and then continue around the east side of the summit through overgrown trail to reach the caves on the north side of the summit block.

La Jolla Valley: Large remote grassland on the western end of the trail. The La Jolla Valley Walk-in Camp sits in this vast meadow, and there is a vernal pond south of the campground. There used to be a 2.3-mile shortcut from the campground to the Ray Miller Trailhead through the valley and La Jolla Canyon, but rock fall in the canyon has closed the trail.

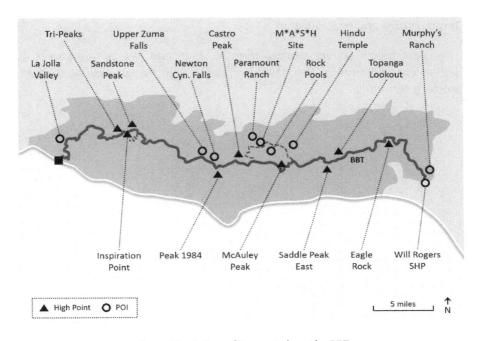

Figure 20 – Points of Interest along the BBT

c. Weather

The BBT lies in perennially sunny Southern California. The elevations only reach as high as 3,111 feet at Sandstone Peak, so don't expect alpine conditions. The heat and sun can be both a burden and a blessing. You can get away with carrying much less cold weather gear, but the blazing sun can torment you just as much as a biting hail storm or freezing wind. Don't be surprised if you check the forecast for your hiking days and see a week of sunshine straight. That's not to say it never rains, but when it does, you may be grateful for a break from the sun.

The best time to hike for weather would be anything outside of the summer months. June, July, August, and even early September will most likely be persistent heat and sun. Although doable, it may be best to schedule your hike outside of these months for more pleasant hiking weather. The best time to hike for wildflowers would be in the springtime, although wildflowers can start as soon as late February. Expect a greater possibility of precipitation in the spring and winter months, but still pleasant conditions. Temperatures and storms are fairly predictable in this region, so if the forecast is calling for rare rainy and cold weather, you can probably count on it.

Temperature and Precipitation

The chart below shows average monthly high and low temperatures as well as precipitation for the Naval Air Station Point Mugu, just west of the western terminus.

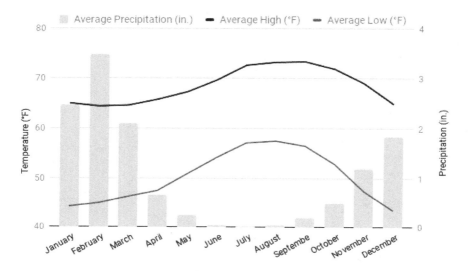

Source: National Oceanic & Atmospheric Administration's monthly climate normals data.

Figure 21 – Average Temperatures and Precipitation (Point Mugu)

d. Camping

The following section includes all pertinent information for planning your campsites along the BBT, including distances, elevations, amenities, and booking information. Due to the limited available camping, several off-trail options are also presented.

Regulations

Camping is restricted to established campsites. Some campsites shown on trail maps may be group camping only, such as Danielson Ranch and Circle X Ranch, but depending on availability may allow solo or small groups of hikers. Malibu Creek State Park has a reservation system through *ReserveAmerica.com* but also allows walk-in camping if spots are available.

Walk-in campgrounds, such as Musch Trail Camp and La Jolla Valley Walk-in, are first-come, first-served sites where payment is done using an envelope system at the campsite, or trailhead in the case of La Jolla Valley. Fires and wood gathering are prohibited. Dogs are allowed on a leash at National Park Service sites, like Circle X Ranch, but no dogs are allowed at California State Parks.

Established Campsites

Since there are only a few campsites along the trail, there is a good chance you will be using most of them. There are subtle differences between them, but generally they are easy to reserve and have simple rules you would expect at a campground.

The distances between these sites make hiking the Backbone Trail a challenge, as they are not evenly spaced along the path. There is a large gap between Malibu Creek State Park Campground and Circle X Ranch (31.4 miles including mileage off the BBT to reach the camps), which is not a reasonable distance to cover in one day for most people. Cleft of the Rock Ranch is one option in that area, but if that still does not align with your hiking itinerary and desired mileages, use one of the many road crossings between Malibu Creek State Park Campground and Circle X Ranch to access the off-trail suggestions provided below via mobile app ride service or other ride service.

The following is a list of campsites from east to west along the BBT:

Musch Trail Camp

Location:	9.9 miles from Will Rogers Trailhead
Details:	Walk-in site with 7-8 campsites, water, bathroom, sink, picnic tables, and horse corrals. $7/night, bring exact change. Pay at the self-registration station on site. No fires allowed. The ground is very tough at some of the sites so bring strong tent stakes if you require them.

Malibu Creek State Park

Location:	Trail to campground is 23.6 miles from Will Rogers Trailhead. Camp is 1.9 miles N off trail.
Details:	Water, restrooms, parking, trash cans, camp host on site during the summer months. $45/night, reservations through *ReserveAmerica.com*. There are also group sites at the campground, so make sure to reserve the appropriate site on the website (standard tent site) or you will be charged the group rate. Walk-in sites available on first-come, first-served basis.

Figure 22 – Musch Trail Camp | Malibu Creek State Park Camp

Cleft of the Rock Ranch (CRR)

Location:	Mulholland Highway. 41.5 miles from Will Rogers Trailhead and 25.3 miles from Ray Miller Trailhead.
Details:	I had the pleasure of staying at Cleft of the Rock Ranch during my most recent hike of the BBT. They offer camping to BBT hikers at their beautiful, secluded property in the mountains not far from the trail, where you will have more privacy than at most of the official campgrounds along the route. This is a huge help to span the distance between Malibu Creek State Park and Circle X Ranch without having to coordinate a ride to off-trail lodging. If they are not available on the days you will be hiking through, the closest campground east, Malibu Creek, is a 19.8-mile walk, and the closest west, Circle X Ranch, is an 11.6-mile walk. That said, consider this a blessing to hikers and think of those who will come after you along the trail. You represent the hiking community, so leave a good impression! Water is available on site. Email *CleftOfTheRockRanch@gmail.com* with your estimated time of arrival to check for availability.

Circle X Ranch

Location:	Trail to ranch is 15.8 miles from Ray Miller Trailhead. Camp is 2.1 miles off trail, head SW at Sandstone Peak Trail junction with Mishe Mokwa connector trail.
Details:	Water, restrooms, parking, trash cans, telephone, and ranger station nearby. Dogs allowed on leash. $35/night, reservations through *Recreation.gov*. Requires groups of at least 10 people, but if you call the National Park Service at +1 (805) 370-2301, they may let you camp there depending on availability. Check closer to the date of your hike, provide a specific date of arrival, and mention that you are thru-hiking the BBT for a better chance of being permitted to camp. Side trail leads 1.5 miles south to *The Grotto*, ending at a lush, secluded waterfall.

Danielson Ranch

Location:	8 miles from Ray Miller Trailhead at the bottom of the climb up to Sandstone Peak
Details:	Water, bathroom, picnic area, trash cans, horse corral. Group site only, but it can be empty on occasion. Contact the state park by emailing *lee.hawkins@ parks.ca.gov*, and you may be allowed to camp depending on availability. Check closer to the date of your hike, provide a specific date of arrival, and mention you are thru-hiking the BBT for a better chance of being permitted to camp. La Jolla Valley Walk-in Camp is a nearby option if you can't camp at Danielson, but there is no water there.

La Jolla Valley Walk-in Camp

Location:	4.6 miles from Ray Miller Trailhead, then 0.4 miles west off trail (easy grade).
Details:	Walk-in site that has picnic tables with lockers but no other facilities. $10/night, pay station at Ray Miller Trailhead parking area. No water! Pit toilet available at western camping area. Secluded spot under oak trees surrounded by large meadows. This campground is rarely used, so there is a good chance a spot will be available. No fires. Also referred to as La Jolla Canyon Walk-In on some trail signs.

Thornhill Broome Beach

Location:	Western Terminus, Ray Miller Trailhead
Details:	Restrooms, water, RV camping, trash cans, and usually a camp host on site. $35/night, reservations are through *ReserveAmerica.com*. Search "Point Mugu SP", select Point Mugu SP, and select the Thornhill Broome sites after clicking "Check Availability". Easy to find, just walk to the ocean from the Ray Miller Trailhead.

Figure 23 – La Jolla Valley Walk-in Camp | Thornhill Broome Beach

Off Trail (Public)

Leo Carrillo Hike and Bike Camp

Location:	20 min. drive from BBT at Latigo Canyon Rd (Mile 33.1); 15 min. drive from Kanan Dume Rd (Mile 35.4), Encinal Canyon Rd (Mile 40.3), or Mulholland Hwy (Mile 41.3); 7 min. drive from PCH/Trancas Canyon bus stop in Malibu.
Details:	Water, restrooms, shower, camp store (summer only), and beach access. The hike and bike camp is located near the park entrance at the PCH and Mulholland Highway. The beach is a short walk across the PCH. $10/night. First-come, first-served. If no hike and bike campsites are available, the regular campsites are $45/night. Reserve at *ReserveAmerica.com*. 35000 W Pacific Coast Hwy, Malibu, CA 90265.

Navy Getaways Point Mugu Beach Hotel and RV Park

Location:	4.6 miles west of Ray Miller Trailhead along PCH on Naval Base Ventura County
Details:	Thornhill Broome Beach camping will be more convenient to the Ray Miller Trailhead, but if that is full, the Point Mugu Beach Hotel and RV Park has tent sites right on the beach inside the Naval base. Open to members of the military (active duty, retired, DOD civilians) and civilian guests, no foreign nationals. The tent sites are just east of the hotel and RV area, where the Mugu Lagoon meets the ocean. Solitude might be broken up by buzzing military aircraft. Closed February 15 through May 30 for seal pup birthing. Tent sites $10/night. +1 (877) NAVY-BED (628-9233) for reservations and +1 (805) 989-8407 for local updates and information. 774 Laguna Rd, NAS Point Mugu, CA 93042.

Off Trail (Private)

Malibu Beach RV Park

Location:	15 min. drive from BBT at Corral Canyon Rd (Mile 28.9); 20 min. drive from Latigo Canyon Rd (Mile 33.1); 10 min. drive from Kanan Dume Rd (Mile 35.4); 20 min. drive from Encinal Canyon Rd (Mile 40.3); 25 min. drive from Mulholland Hwy (Mile 41.5)
Details:	East of the City of Malibu along the Pacific Coast Highway. Tent sites are $40/night off-season (October-May) and $50/night during the busy season (June-September). 25801 Pacific Coast Highway, Malibu, CA 90265. +1 (800) 622-6052. Maliburv.com.

Vacation Rentals, various locations

The BBT intersects the Santa Monica Mountains just a few miles from one of the most-populous cities in the U.S., Los Angeles, and shares a zip code with some of its wealthiest residents. There are private homes throughout the mountains and many are available to be rented out for weekend getaways. Use the road crossings between Malibu Creek Campground and Circle X Ranch to access these rentals for a night off the trail and break up the 31.6 miles between camps.

You can browse rental options on sites like AirBnB, HomeAway, etc. by searching "Malibu" as your location. Use the map display to compare available properties to a map of the BBT. You also may want to filter out all the luxury rental properties by setting an upper limit to your desired price range in the search options. If your budget is unlimited, there are some amazing properties available as vacation rentals.

[!] Use caution when contacting someone off the internet and giving away personal or financial information. Rental websites attempt to vet and verify accounts, but check reviews for your host to make sure a few people have stayed with them and had a good experience.

Cell service is usually available at road crossings or within a few miles of a road crossing to schedule rides to any off-trail locations.

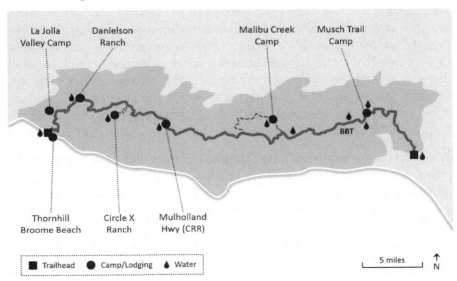

Figure 24 – Campgrounds and Water Locations along the BBT

The table below lists all campgrounds on the BBT along with their cumulative miles from the Will Rogers State Historic Park trailhead.

Campground	Distance (mi)	Cumulative (mi)	Elevation (ft)
Musch Trail Camp	9.9	9.9	1,316
Malibu Creek State Park (1.9 mi N at Tapia Park Trailhead)	13.7	23.6	490
Mulholland Highway (CRR)	17.9	41.5	1,621
Circle X Ranch (2.1 mi SW at BBT junction with Sandstone Peak Trail)	9.5	51	2,297
Danielson Ranch	7.8	58.8	300
La Jolla Valley Walk-in (0.5 mi N)	3.4	62.2	932
Thornhill Broome Beach (0.4 mi S at Ray Miller Trailhead)	5.0	67.2	33

Table 7 – Distances between Campgrounds on the BBT

e. Water

Do not expect to find water from a natural source along the trail. Water is only reliably available from established campgrounds and facilities. Take advantage of the potable water provided at these locations and assume that will be the only water available to you until you reach the next site.

Plan to start the hike with your pack filled to capacity with water. There are several stretches of over 10 miles between water sources, including one stretch from Tapia Park (Malibu Creek Campground access point) to Circle X Ranch of about 30 miles between water sources. If possible, a water cache at one of the many road crossings in this area would be incredibly valuable to save weight in your pack and ensure you have all the water you need. However, the National Park Service is opposed to caches while the California State Park is more lenient, so cache at your own risk.

The good thing about water along the BBT is that, since it is always from a piped potable water source, there is virtually no situation where you will need to treat your water, allowing you to save weight on water treatment gear. There is no need to carry anything more than water treatment drops in case of emergency and even that might be overkill. In any water emergency, you will be more concerned with finding water than how to treat it.

Plan on carrying and drinking a lot of water to stay hydrated through the steep, sun-exposed climbs on the BBT. A rough rule of thumb for how much water to carry between sources is one liter (about one quart or 34 fl. oz.)

per 2-3 miles. If your pack is light and you are comfortable with miles, maybe you can bump that up to 5 miles per liter, but start out conservative and adjust as you progress along the BBT.

Make note of how much water you have left over when you get to the next source. The goal is to carry only a little bit more water than you need. Water, weighing 2.2 pounds per liter, can be the heaviest item in your pack at times. It is obviously lifesaving and essential, but carrying too much can wear you out. Don't just carry the water, drink it while hiking. Get the weight off your back and stay hydrated. Drink lots of water at each water source to ensure you are hydrated before heading out to the next source. The most I carried on the BBT was 6 liters.

The table below lists all reliable water sources on the BBT along with their cumulative miles from Will Rogers State Historic Park and distance to the next water source (see also Figure 25 above). All sources are potable. There are no reliable natural sources on the BBT, except for Malibu Creek. However, it is not recommended to drink from Malibu Creek. There are many potable piped water sources available in that area as an alternative.

Water Source	Distance (mi)	Cumulative (mi)	Elevation (ft)
Will Rogers State Historic Park	0	0	433
Musch Trail Camp via Eagle Rock	9.9	9.9	1,316
Trippet Ranch (0.1 mi S) via Musch Trail Camp	0.9	10.8	1,195
Dead Horse Trailhead at Topanga Canyon Blvd	1.2	12	850
Tapia Park Trailhead (Restroom sink or in Tapia Park 0.2 mi N)	11.6	23.6	490
Mulholland Highway (CRR)	17.9	41.5	1,621
Trail to Circle X Ranch (2.1 mi SW)	9.5	51	2,297
Danielson Ranch	7.8	58.8	300
Ray Miller Trailhead	8	66.8	33

Table 8 – Distances between Water Sources on the BBT

f. Flora & Fauna

To walk the BBT is to tour the native plant communities of the Santa Monica Mountains. Dense shrubby chaparral, shady oaklands, and aromatic sage scrub lands thrive in the coastal Mediterranean climate with cool, wet winters and bone-dry summers. These communities are made up of drought-tolerant evergreen plants that have a winter growing season, when most of the rain falls. This diverse and unique landscape is home to many creatures. The following section presents a few examples of the species that call these mountains home but is nowhere near comprehensive. See *Links & References* section of the appendix for recommended reading.

Vegetation

- **Redshank or ribbonwood.** Wispy emerald green shrub with red strips of bark falling off the trunk that seems to look lush no matter how long it has waited for rain. Their presence around Sandstone Peak and Boney Mountain make that hike a special place. Similar to the shorter, duller, and more prevalent chamise.

- **Coast live oak.** Inviting oaks will be your respite from the blazing sun. The clearings under their huge canopies are perfect for rest and relaxation.

Figure 25 – Redshank Crown | Oak Tree Shade

- **Manzanita.** Shrub with pale, round leaves and maroon bark that is unbelievably smooth. Manzanita groves line the trail at many points.

- **California sycamore.** Huge sycamores fill the canyons of the Santa Monica Mountains. Around Danielson Ranch in Sycamore Canyon are some great examples of the size these native Californians can reach. Patchy pale bark with huge leaves and long arms stretching and bending, sometimes downwards.

- **Sagebrush.** Found throughout the chaparral and coastal sage scrub communities. Their fragrance emanates through these sections.

- **Chalk liveforever.** Succulent with pale, waxy coating on its leaves and tall stems that protrude from the rosette.

- **Yucca.** Easily identified by the ball of long, spiny leaves with sharp points at the base of this flowering plant. Once the plant reaches maturity, around 5 to 10 years, a single flower stem emerges from the base and grows up to ten feet high in a short amount of time. After a display of white and purple flowers, the yucca dies and leaves behind a skeleton of the spiny base and flower stalk for years. Green flower buds are edible but very bitter.

Figure 26 – Chalk Liveforever | California Poppy | Slender Mariposa Lily

- **Wildflowers** include morning glory, lupine, bush monkey flower, California poppy, wooly blue-curl, blue dicks, Parry's phacelia, slender Mariposa lily, and Indian paintbrush. However, there are hundreds of wildflower species found along the trail. If you are hiking in the springtime, you will see a fair amount.

[i] The National Park Service has created the *Santa Monica Mountains Flower Finder* app to identify wildflowers based on color, size, season, and other identifying factors. Search using the keywords "smm wildflowers mobile" on your phone and you should be redirected to the app download or a mobile version of the flower finder. Additionally, they maintain a wildflower report that documents where and when flowers have been seen as the season progresses.

Link: *http://www.smmflowers.org/whatsblooming*

Wildlife

More than 450 species of vertebrate call the Santa Monica Mountains home. Many times, you will be walking and sense little signs of life all around you. Lizards scurry away as you crunch through the trail, towhees chirp from the low brush, and flycatchers dart past branches with amazing agility. As you walk through the mountains, the wildlife along the Backbone Trail seems unfazed by the large metropolis at their doorstep, but their resilience has been tested for a long time and will continue to be without conservation efforts.

- **Coyote.** These canines have become increasingly well-adjusted to the urban environment of Los Angeles. However, they still roam the wilderness of the Santa Monica Mountains. You may hear their distinct yipping call as you settle in for the night.

- **Mountain lion.** A small mountain lion population calls the Santa Monica Mountains home. You would be extremely lucky to see one. The population is restricted to the Santa Monica Mountains by the Pacific Ocean to the south and the 101 freeway to the north. A proposed wildlife crossing of freeway 101 would expand these lions' range north and provide some relief to the population.

- **Bobcat.** Very rare, spotted cats. Much smaller than mountain lions and not as dangerous to humans. I was lucky enough to watch one hunt at the Malibu Creek State Park Campground.

Figure 27 – Bobcat at Malibu Creek Camp | Ground Squirrel

- **Southern Pacific rattlesnake.** Venomous snake found throughout the mountains. They seek shade in the daytime and come out in the evening or mornings to hunt. They hibernate in the wintertime. Be careful around boulders casting shade or ditches, where a snake may be hiding in the daytime.

Other common species include red-tailed hawk, Anna's hummingbird, California quail, and coast horned lizard.

g. Safety

The BBT does not have many high-risk situations that one might encounter along the route. However, it does not hurt to be aware of all possible scenarios. Some safety issues include the following:

Travel will feel safe along the BBT. You are surprisingly secluded for being so close to a major population center. That said, there are a lot of people that use these mountains on a daily basis. You will see other people out on the trail, at the major road crossings, and in some of the campgrounds, especially Malibu Creek State Park. If you get lost, you are always a day's walk from a population center or road, usually only a few hours' walk. Cell service is available on a surprising amount of the Santa Monica Mountains as well. It is unlikely you will get lost to a point where you will be in danger.

Some road crossings can be hazardous. There will not be a pedestrian crossing at most roads. Cars can travel very fast on the winding mountain roads and drivers do not have much of a reaction time due to some of the bends on these roads. Exercise extreme caution when crossing roads.

Figure 28 – Road Crossing | Black-Legged Tick

Several wild animals and plants pose a risk in the Santa Monica Mountains. Be respectful and alert in their presence. Mountain lions, while rare, do live in the Santa Monica Mountains and have attacked humans. If you come across a mountain lion, do not approach it. Make yourself as large as possible by lifting things over your head. Give the mountain lion the opportunity to leave the area. Do not run or crouch. Try to scare the lion by waving your arms, yelling, or grabbing large objects nearby. If attacked or threatened, throw rocks or sticks and fight back.

Similar to the TCT, rattlesnakes, ticks, and poison oak pose potential safety hazards on the BBT. Do your best to avoid any contact and follow the advice given in Section 2g to handle possible encounters appropriately. The same applies to the advice given for dealing with the constant sun exposure, which is to be expected in the Santa Monica Mountains as well.

The BBT goes through several well-travelled areas along its route, many with cell phone service, but there are also solitary sections of the trail where you may not see another person for miles. Satellite communicators would add an extra level of safety. However, they are not essential. Always share your itinerary with a 3rd party and update them with your location when possible.

In the case of emergency, always call 911. Cell service may not always be available so, if possible, send one person for help while at least one person remains with the victim. Getting to road crossings and campgrounds will increase your chances of finding someone who can call for help or reach cell phone service.

- Malibu Urgent Care Center at 23656 Pacific Coast Highway, Malibu, CA 90265 is open daily from 9:00 AM to 7:00 PM. Phone number: +1 (310) 456-7551.

- Los Robles Hospital and Medical Center in Thousand Oaks is at 215 West Janes Road, Thousand Oaks, CA 91360. Phone number: +1 (805) 497-2727.

h. Other Conditions

Generally, the weather in the Santa Monica Mountains is stable and pleasant. However, it can be susceptible to some extreme environmental and meteorological conditions. The area has been under a drought for several years, making it more susceptible to wildfires and landslides. Contact the National Park Service at +1 (805) 370-2301 and California State Parks at +1 (818) 880-0363 before heading out for information on closures and conditions.

4. Long Lead Items

The following section provides information useful during the advanced planning stages for hiking either of the trails, including permits, finding a hiking partner, and making travel arrangements.

a. Permits

Trans-Catalina Trail

Permits are free and included with your camping reservation. Your camping reservation provides your approximate location to the Catalina Island Conservancy in case of an emergency, such as a wildfire, and a separate hiking permit would not provide any additional information, so they do not require it. Perhaps if the trail starts getting overcrowded, they will regulate the number of hikers on the TCT, but as of right now that is not the case. There is no need to register for a hiking permit or carry a permit with you on the trail if you have made camping reservations.

[i] If you will be day-hiking out of Two Harbors or Avalon, then a hiking permit is required and is available for free online at *www.catalina conservancy.org/community*.

Make sure to check in for your campsites your first day on the island by calling the Two Harbors Visitor Center at +1 (310) 510-4205, if you are starting from Avalon, or visit them in Two Harbors at the foot of the ferry dock. They are open from 8:00 AM to 4:00 PM, seven days a week. This is important for locating hikers in the backcountry in case of an emergency on the island, so please check in early before arriving at your campsite. Consider this the actual "permit" to hike the TCT.

Backbone Trail

There is no permit required for the BBT either. The trail crosses through federal and state park lands but, thankfully, neither require permits for hiking. If they did that would seriously hinder the many people who recreate in the Santa Monica Mountains on a daily basis.

Camping regulations apply, but you don't need a permit in advance for camping. Just make sure you pay for your site if you are using a walk-in campsite, such as Musch Trail Camp or La Jolla Valley Walk-in, or pay in advance for sites like Malibu Creek State Park and Circle X Ranch.

In the future, as backcountry camps are added along the route, a permit system is likely to be enacted. As of the publishing of this book, the National Park Service claims that "thru-hiking is not possible at this time" due to the limited number of campgrounds. Therefore, they do not require permits nor do California State Parks.

b. Hiking Partner

Backpacking the entire length of a route is a rewarding and challenging experience that can be enhanced, or hindered, by the presence of a hiking partner. A hiking partner is not necessary for either the TCT or BBT, but you may be thinking of someone, or a group, you would like to have along with you to share this experience. Reach out to friends early on during your planning to improve the chance of finding someone who can set aside the time for a multi-day hike.

Hiking with Others

Consider your own fitness against that of any potential hiking partners. Is this someone that is going to run circles around you? Is this someone that will make you struggle to meet your daily mileage? It is very important to have compatible fitness levels. Keep in mind that just because one person hikes at a slower pace on the trail doesn't mean they can't cover the same distance in a day as you. Many times, I have hiked with a partner who I may not hike side-by-side with, but we meet up at water sources, campgrounds, and nice resting places to catch up and share the moment. As long as someone is not having to wait an excessive amount of time at breaks, then you should be fine. Actually, you may find it a little annoying to always have someone on your heels and that you enjoy space while walking with the peace of mind that your friend or friends are right around the corner somewhere.

Almost as important as compatible fitness levels are compatible agendas for the hike. Make sure you and any potential hiking partners agree about the pace and goals of the hike. Are you interested in pushing the miles to challenge yourself or do you want to check out every side trail and spend as long as possible on the trail? Will you be taking time to do activities other than hiking, such as reading, writing, photography, swimming, etc.? Are there scheduling constraints that will force one person to hike the trail in a certain number of days and does that still work for everyone? You can hike these trails as slow or as fast as you want, but make sure everyone is on the same page before heading out together.

Another aspect to consider is gear sharing and overall planning. You can save weight in your pack by sharing a shelter, stove and fuel, water treatment (although not necessary on these trails), and food. But make sure you both are carrying basic first aid, maps, and water in case you get separated for a significant amount of time. Sharing gear makes you reliant on your partner. If your hiking partner gets off the trail, you must carry all the shared gear yourself or get off the trail with them. If you are hiking with a close friend or significant other who you don't plan on hiking without, this approach is recommended. If you are hiking in a large group or with someone you don't know that well, then maybe consider planning independently. Sharing gear can complicate the planning process, and if someone bails at the last minute, you have to find new gear.

Hiking with others also has a level of safety built in that hiking alone does not. In emergency situations, you are more likely to have someone that can start to address the emergency immediately and provide aid or seek help. Also, having a hiking partner can help address smaller emergencies, like when you forget to bring toothpaste and can borrow some from your buddy.

Finally, it is always fun to introduce your friends to new experiences, and backpacking is no different. If someone is willing to get out of their comfort zone and try something new, don't look past that because you are worried they can't keep up or won't be 100% ready with all the appropriate gear. Yes, you may have to go through their pack and throw out that extra pair of jeans they thought they needed, but little things like that will be worth it if you have a new hiking partner for life, who can thank you for introducing them to this wonderful lifestyle.

Hiking Solo

Planning and hiking a trail alone will enable a simpler experience and most likely increase the distance you cover every day. When you are alone, you tend to hike more often, take less and shorter breaks, and don't feel the anxiety of whether you are hiking too fast or too slow for your partner. If you want to spend extra time at a lunch break, you can do that without feeling like you're holding someone up. If you want to night-hike, go for it! You are only responsible for yourself. This freedom and responsibility is wonderful and can enhance the feeling of accomplishment and level of confidence instilled at the end of the hike, knowing you did it yourself. Heading out solo can be intimidating but extremely rewarding in ways you may not be able to anticipate.

c. Travel Arrangements

All trailheads and ferry ports, except for the Ray Miller Trailhead, are within the Los Angeles metropolitan area and accessible through a combination of public transportation options. Several are presented below for travel from LAX, the main international airport for the area, and Union Station in downtown L.A., the main train station for the area. It is possible to use mobile mapping applications or web-based navigation services to find public transportation options if your travel does not originate from one of these two major transportation hubs.

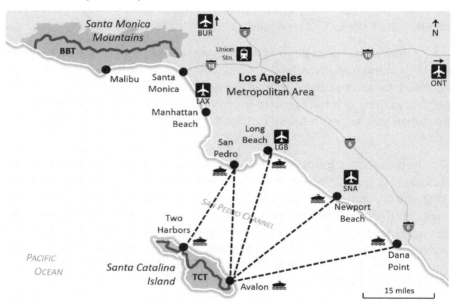

Figure 29 – Travel Options for TCT & BBT

If you are travelling from outside the Los Angeles area, check travel to and from the following locations:

Airports

Los Angeles International Airport (LAX) is not far from the starting points for either the TCT or BBT and will give you the most options for flights and likely the best prices. John Wayne Orange County Airport (SNA), Long Beach Airport (LGB; closest to mainland ports for the Catalina ferries), Ontario International Airport (ONT), and Burbank Bob Hope Airport (BUR) all service the area as well, but options for flights are more limited.

Train Stations

Amtrak connects to Union Station in downtown Los Angeles as well as points in Orange County. You can take local trains ($1.75) from Union Station to Long Beach or Santa Monica to get closer to the TCT ferry ports and BBT trailheads, respectively.

Travel to the Trans-Catalina Trail

Check availability of ferries and campgrounds early for Catalina in case it is during a busy weekend. Your other travel arrangements will likely hinge on the ferry schedules. Ferry times vary, and if you want an early start out of Avalon, only Long Beach offers 6:00 AM departures to the island (roughly a 1-hour ride). Also, from October 25th to April 6th, no ferries run in or out of Two Harbors on Tuesdays and Thursdays. Only San Pedro has service to Two Harbors.

TCT Ferry Ports

- Long Beach: 320 Golden Shore, Long Beach, CA 90802
- San Pedro: Berth 95, San Pedro, CA 90731
- Dana Point: 34675 Golden Lantern Street, Dana Point, CA 92629
- Newport Beach: Balboa Pavilion, 400 Main Street, Newport Beach, CA 92661

Drive

- LAX to San Pedro/Long Beach: 30 minutes
- Union Station to San Pedro/Long Beach: 30-45 minutes
- Long Beach Airport to Long Beach ferry port: 15 minutes

Shuttle or Bus

- Karmel Shuttle (+1 (888)-995-7433) and Sav-On Shuttle (+1 (800) 642-0167) service a range of locations, including LAX and Long Beach/San Pedro ports, and are recommended by the Catalina Chamber of Commerce.
- There is also an Amtrak-dedicated bus route, California Thruway Bus, from Union Station to Long Beach and San Pedro. Purchase California Thruway bus tickets ($15) by selecting San Pedro as your destination when you buy your rail tickets.

Rideshare Service Rates

- LAX to San Pedro/Long Beach: $25-$34

- Union Station to San Pedro/Long Beach: $25-$35

Public Transportation

<u>LAX to Long Beach:</u>

LAX FlyAway bus (www.lawa.org/FlyAway) will take you directly from any LAX terminal (look for green signs at ground transportation) to Long Beach (50 minutes). Purchase tickets in advance online. You will be dropped off at 1st Street and Long Beach Boulevard, a 0.9 mile walk to the Catalina Express Long Beach ferry port. Your options are to walk the remaining 0.9 miles or walk one block west on 1st Street to Promenade Square and catch the Long Beach Transit 121 bus, which will take you directly to the ferry port at 320 Golden Shore (10 minutes). Estimated time: 1 hour 10 minutes. Cost $10.25 ($9 for LAX FlyAway bus to Long Beach, $1.25 for Long Beach Transit 121 bus).

<u>Union Station to Long Beach:</u>

Go downstairs to the Metro Rail platforms. Take the Red or Purple line to the 7th St/Metro Center Stop (5 minutes) and transfer to the Blue Line by walking upstairs to the Long Beach-bound Blue Line trains, indicated by a dark blue circle. Be sure not to board Blue Line trains to Santa Monica, which have a similar-looking light blue circle with a capital-letter "E" in the middle. Take the Metro Blue Line to Downtown Long Beach (1 hour). Upon exiting the Downtown Long Beach station, you are a 0.6-mile walk from the Catalina Express ferry port. Your options are to walk the remaining 0.6 miles or transfer to the Long Beach Transit 121 bus on Pacific Ave outside of the Metro Rail station in front of the Long Beach Public Library, which will take you directly to the ferry port at 320 Golden Shore. If you will be taking the Long Beach Transit 121 bus, purchase a Metro to MUNI Transfer at Union Station when paying for your rail fare and you will be able to board the 121 bus without paying another fare. Estimated time: 1 hour 30 minutes. Cost $2.25 ($1.75 for Metro Rail, $0.50 for Metro to MUNI Transfer to Long Beach Transit).

Ferry Details

Catalina Express:

Services both Avalon and Two Harbors out of Long Beach, San Pedro, and Dana Point on the mainland. Offers the most options for times and locations. $72 round-trip, check website for schedules. You can change your reservation at no charge up until 6:00 PM the day before your trip, depending on availability. +1 (800) 613-1212; *www.catalinaexpress.com*

Catalina Flyer:

Once a day from Newport Beach to Avalon and back. $70 round-trip, 9:00 AM out of Newport and 4:30 PM out of Avalon. +1 (949) 673-5245; *www.catalinainfo.com*

Some Avalon hotels will offer package deals for the room and ferry fare. There are daily trips from the mainland via San Pedro, Long Beach, Dana Point, and Newport Beach to Avalon. However, only San Pedro also services Two Harbors. If you are planning on hiking from Avalon to Two Harbors, or vice versa, and leaving a car parked on the mainland, only San Pedro gives you the option to return to the same point. Long Beach is only a 6-mile drive from San Pedro and with a little extra walking also accessible using the LADOT Commuter Express 142 bus.

Additionally, ferry departure times out of San Pedro may not sync up with your hiking itinerary. The earliest ferry from San Pedro to Avalon arrives at 10:00 AM. It will be difficult to hike the almost 16 miles to Blackjack Campground from Avalon on the first day starting at 10:00 AM. Dana Point and Newport Beach ferries also don't arrive until around 10:00 AM in Avalon. Only Long Beach offers an early ferry, arriving at 7:00 AM.

Options to help cover the almost 16 miles to Blackjack Campground out of Avalon and make it back to a vehicle on the mainland include:

- Take the early ferry out of Long Beach to Avalon, which arrives at 7:00 AM, hike the TCT to Two Harbors, then take the ferry from Two Harbors to San Pedro. Take a taxi, rideshare, or bus for the 6 miles to your car at the Long Beach terminal.

- Get a ride (from a friend, taxi, rideshare, or public transportation) to and from the mainland ports. You have the freedom to choose your schedule without worrying about returning to a vehicle.

- Shortcut out of Avalon by taking the Hermit Gulch Trail and save 5 miles on the hike to Blackjack Campground.

- Stay one night in Avalon, either at a hotel or Hermit Gulch Campground. This allows you to either break up the first section to Blackjack Campground into two halves (hiking the far eastern portion then back into Avalon for a night, then out again the next day straight to Blackjack) or start early the following morning giving you plenty of time to make it to Blackjack.

- Take the Safari Bus from Two Harbors to Avalon ($57; schedule varies depending on time of year) at the end of your hike, then take a ferry out of Avalon to the port where your car is parked.

- Start the TCT at Two Harbors (must depart from San Pedro), from which Parsons' Landing, Two Harbors, and Little Harbor Campgrounds are all under 10 miles away.

[!] If you are planning on hiking during Catalina's "off season", between October and April, then ferries may not be running at all some days of the week, depending on the ports you use. Check the ferry schedule early in the planning stage and again once you have a target date to ensure the timing is correct for your first day of hiking.

Additionally, no flammable substances are allowed on the ferries, which would include your camp stove fuel. The Two Harbors General Store has a wide variety of fuel available, but no denatured alcohol or Heet®. Chet's Hardware in Avalon (open 8:00 AM to 5:00 PM) has isobutane/propane fuel canisters and denatured alcohol in a 16-ounce container.

Island Transportation

Island transportation services can take you from Two Harbors to Avalon, as well as several other locations on the island, such as Little Harbor, the Catalina Airport (aka Airport in the Sky), and Blackjack Campground. You could use these services to facilitate a section hike of the TCT or simply shorten the hike to fit your schedule.

Shuttle Services

<u>Wildlands Express:</u>

Out of Avalon for travel to the airport only. It has a more frequent schedule than the Safari Bus, which also goes to the airport. $16 one way to the airport. Call +1 (310) 510-0143 for reservations and information.

Safari Bus:

Out of Avalon and Two Harbors and connects Two Harbors, Little Harbor, the airport, and Avalon via interior roads. There are frequent daily trips between Two Harbors and Little Harbor, but it travels only once a day between Two Harbors and Avalon, so check the schedule to be sure it works with your ferry times and hiking itinerary. A one-way trip from Two Harbors to Avalon takes about 2 hours. Cost is $25 for Two Harbors to Little Harbor, $16 for Little Harbor to the airport, and $16 for the airport to Avalon. Each leg must be booked individually, so a Two Harbors to Avalon trip would be $57 for one person. Two Harbors to Little Harbor is booked through Two Harbors Visitor Services at +1 (310) 510-4205. All other travel is booked through the airport at +1 (310) 510-0143. They also have charter shuttles, which may be more affordable for large groups.

Catalina Transportation Services:

Local Avalon taxi service to the eastern terminus, Hermit Gulch Campground, Wrigley Memorial, and other points around Avalon. They offer specialized shuttle services from Avalon to some of the same island interior locations, as well as Parsons' Landing, in less time than the Safari Bus and Wildlands Express, but for a much higher fee. Interior shuttles would be good for groups, since they can carry up to seven people with luggage, and splitting the fare will be cheaper than individual Safari Bus or Wildlands Express tickets. Call +1 (310) 510-0025 to schedule taxi pickups and +1 (310) 510-0342 for more information on interior shuttles.

Avalon Bus:

There is a city bus route in Avalon, called the Garibaldi, which goes around Avalon and up to Hermit Gulch Campground and the Wrigley Memorial garden. $1 per ride. You need to switch buses to get up to Hermit Gulch and Wrigley Memorial and Botanic Garden. Visit *http://www.cityofavalon.com/* transit for schedule and route info.

Catalina Backcountry:

Provides coordination between many services available on the island. If something you desire does not fit into the island services listed above, Catalina Backcountry may be able to accommodate you. They can facilitate your hike by scheduling gear hauls, grocery shopping, reserving hotels before or after the hike, and anything else you might want along the TCT. Think of them as your own travel agent for the TCT. If there is some special request or arrangement you have, this would be the place to look. Call +1 (310) 913-9036 for more information.

Boat

An interesting option to avoid backtracking to Two Harbors on the island's west end is to take a boat to Parsons' Landing or Emerald Bay near Parsons' Landing. You would still have to hike the 4.6 miles from Parsons' Landing to Starlight Beach, the true western terminus of the TCT, and back to Parsons' Landing. Contact the Two Harbors harbor department at +1 (310) 510-4253 and ask for the Two Harbors Shore Boat service in order to get more information on boats to Parsons' Landing or Emerald Bay.

If you want to get creative, you could take a private charter to (or from) Starlight Beach, although that may be difficult, since it is a very rocky beach with no good landing.

Travel to the Backbone Trail

BBT Trailheads

- Eastern Terminus (Will Rogers State Historic Park): 1400 Will Rogers State Park Road, Pacific Palisades, CA 90272
- Western Terminus (Point Mugu State Park): Ray Miller Trailhead, Malibu, CA 90265

Drive

- LAX to Will Rogers Trailhead: 20 minutes; 45 minutes in traffic
- Union Station to Will Rogers Trailhead: 30 minutes; 1 hour in traffic.
- LAX to Ray Miller Trailhead (46 miles): 1 hour; 2 hours in traffic.
- Union Station to Ray Miller Trailhead (50 miles): 1 hour; 2 hours in traffic.

Rideshare Service Rates

- LAX to Will Rogers Trailhead: $26-$34
- Union Station to Will Rogers Trailhead: $23-$31
- LAX to Ray Miller Trailhead: $54-$71
- Union Station to Ray Miller Trailhead: $51-$68

Public Transportation

<u>LAX to Will Rogers Trailhead:</u>

Take LAX Shuttle Bus C (blue signs at ground transportation, no fare is required to board this shuttle) from any terminal to Parking Lot C and walk north to the LAX Metro Bus Center, Lot C. Take the Culver City Bus Line 6/6r (for rapid) route to Westwood Blvd and Weyburn Ave (45 minutes). Walk north one block to the Le Conte/Westwood intersection and transfer to the Metro Bus (Los Angeles) Line 2/302. This transfer point is near lots of shopping and grocery stores if you need to pick something up before hitting the trail. The 2/302 Bus will take you right to Will Rogers State Historic Park and a short walk to the trailhead. Get off at the Sunset Blvd and Evans Rd stop (30 minutes) and walk west up the trail and into Will Rogers State Historic Park. You will come upon a polo field. Walk to the west of the field, and the trailhead will be straight ahead between the parking lot and tennis courts, 0.4 miles from the Sunset/Evans bus stop. Estimated time is 1 hour 45 minutes from the LAX Bus Center to the BBT trailhead. Cost $1.40 ($1 for Culver City Bus, $0.40 for transfer). Ask driver for an Interagency Transfer when you pay your fare to board the 2 or 302 Metro Bus. Transfers are good for two hours.

Alternatively, you could take the Santa Monica Big Blue Bus Route 3/Rapid 3 bus from the same LAX Metro Bus Center, Lot C to 4th St and Santa Monica Blvd (35 minutes), right next to an REI and other shopping, then transfer to Route 9 and take that to Chautauqua Blvd, Pampas Ricas Blvd, and Sunset Blvd intersection (20 minutes), where you will transfer to the Metro Bus Line 2/302 and take that to the Sunset/Evans stop (3 minutes). You must continue walking northeast on Sunset Blvd for 0.1 mile to reach the trailhead into Will Rogers State Historic Park on your left. You could also skip the transfer to the Metro Bus Line 2/302 and walk 0.9 miles to the trailhead into Will Rogers State Historic Park, then 0.4 miles to the BBT trailhead. Estimated time is 1 hour 35 minutes. Cost $3 ($1.25 for each Big Blue Bus and $0.50 for Interagency Transfer to the 2/302 Metro Bus).

<u>Union Station to Will Rogers Trailhead:</u>

There is a Metro Bus Line 2/302 stop at Broadway and Cesar E Chavez Ave (0.3 mile walk west from Union Station) that will take you to the Sunset/ Evans bus stop described above. Total estimated time is 2 hours. Cost $1.75.

Ray Miller Trailhead:

Unfortunately, there is no public transportation to the Ray Miller Trailhead. It is possible to take a bus to Trancas Canyon Rd and Pacific Coast Highway in Malibu, which gets you most of the way there, and then use a mobile app rideshare service to get to the trailhead. Mobile app rideshare service from the bus stop in Malibu to Ray Miller Trailhead is about $13-$19. Otherwise, you would need to arrange a ride out to the Ray Miller Trailhead.

From LAX: Take the Santa Monica Big Blue Bus Route 3/Rapid 3 bus from the LAX Metro Bus Center, Lot C as described above to 4th St and Colorado Ave (35 minutes). There are lots of restaurants and shopping in downtown Santa Monica, including an REI. Walk one block northeast on Colorado Ave past the Metro Rail station and half a block southeast on 5th St to the Metro Bus 543 Line. Take the 534 Line to the last stop, west of Malibu, at Trancas Canyon Rd and Pacific Coast Highway (1 hour). There is some shopping and an upscale grocery store in this area. The Ray Miller Trailhead is 12.3 miles west on the Pacific Coast Highway. Leo Carrillo Hike and Bike Camp is 5.3 miles west on the PCH. Estimated time is 1 hour and 45 minutes. Cost is $1.75 ($1.25 for the Big Blue Bus and $0.50 for Interagency Transfer to the 534 Metro Bus).

From Union Station: Go downstairs to the Metro Rail platforms. Take the Red or Purple line to the 7th St/Metro Center Stop (5 minutes) and transfer to the Metro Expo Line by walking upstairs to the Santa Monica-bound Expo Line trains, indicated by a capital "E" enclosed by a light blue circle. Be sure not to board Blue Line trains to Long Beach, which have a similar-looking dark blue circle as their symbol. Take the Metro Expo Line to Downtown Santa Monica (50 minutes), the end of the line. There are lots of restaurants and shopping in downtown Santa Monica, including an REI. Walk to the bus stop on 5th St outside of the rail station. Take the Metro Bus 534 Line to the last stop, west of Malibu, at Trancas Canyon Rd and Pacific Coast Highway (1 hour). There is some shopping and an upscale grocery store in this area. The Ray Miller Trailhead is 12.3 miles west on the Pacific Coast Highway. Leo Carrillo Hike and Bike Camp is 5.3 miles west on the PCH. Estimated time 2 hours 15 minutes. Cost $1.75.

The Trancas Canyon/PCH bus stop is close to the Chumash Indian and Zuma Ridge Trails, which connect to the BBT at mile 38, close to the halfway point in 6.1 miles. The Chumash Indian Trailhead is at latitude, longitude coordinates 34.035094, -118.840025. From the bus stop, walk to the northeast corner of the shopping area onto a dirt footpath heading east and cross Trancas Creek into open space. If Trancas Creek is running high, you may have to cross on the PCH bridge. Follow the dirt paths east for 0.1 miles to a pair of tennis courts and turn north onto a maintenance road along the west side of the tennis courts. Follow that for 0.3 miles, staying left at all junctions, to the unsigned turnoff for the unmaintained Chumash Indian Trail. There may be a small rock cairn indicating the turnoff location. Continue 1.5 miles to the Zuma Ridge Trail and then 4 miles to the BBT.

d. Accommodations

Trans-Catalina Trail

There are many options for lodging and accommodations in Avalon, much less in Two Harbors. The mainland ports of San Pedro, Long Beach, Newport Beach, and Dana Point have hotel options as well, many of which may be more affordable than what is available on Catalina Island. If you do stay in Avalon, your hotel may offer a deal on the ferry ticket.

Backbone Trail

If you are looking for accommodations before or after the trail, you have the entire Los Angeles area to choose from, so the prices and locations will vary greatly. Santa Monica and Malibu are the most convenient towns to the eastern and western trailheads of the BBT, but you may find more affordable options elsewhere, such as the San Fernando Valley or further west in Ventura County.

5. Planning & Preparation

Now that you know what is out there on the trail, you can begin assembling an itinerary, food, and gear to meet the challenge. The following section provides recommendations for developing a hiking plan that would apply for both the TCT and BBT. These are only recommendations, and if you have a system that works for you, feel free to substitute only a few of the ideas from this section. Both trails experience hot and dry weather with a lot of climbing, so planning and preparation should focus on being lightweight to handle these conditions more comfortably.

a. Itinerary

In general, the itinerary planning process can be broken down into two stages. The first stage includes all activities concerning long lead items discussed in the previous chapter, such as permits, hiking partner, and travel arrangements, which create a big picture framework, or 'macro-plan', for the hike. The second stage focuses on the specifics of your thru-hike, such as daily distances and desired campsites. The resulting 'micro-plan' is your personal hiking itinerary.

Macro-Planning

By the end of the macro-planning stage, you should have your start and end dates, travel reservations, and any necessary accommodations after the hike figured out. This is essential if you are travelling from outside of the Los Angeles area and need to reserve plane tickets and hotel rooms. But even local hikers will have to set a date in order to reserve campgrounds and ferry tickets, in the case of the TCT. The following steps will guide you through this stage.

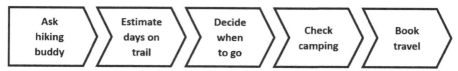

Figure 30 – Macro-Planning Flow Chart

1) Coordinate with potential hiking partners

Determine whether you will be hiking alone or in a group, and then figure out goals on the pace of the hike (aggressive or relaxed).

2) Estimate days on the trail

Figure out a comfortable daily mileage for you, or your group, and compare that to the table in Section 1b to figure out the number of days you will likely be on the trail.

3) Determine desired time of year

Figure out, roughly, what time of year you can hike based on your and any hiking partner's schedule. Now compare that to nature's schedule and select a time of year to hit the trail.

Both trails, being in the same climate, can be scorching in the middle of the summer and have a risk of rain in the winter. Ideally, you would hike in early to mid-March for wildflowers, although any early spring hike should have great wildflowers and temperatures. Fall will have mild temperatures, but plant life won't be as vibrant.

4) Check camping availability

All campsites, except for Musch Trail and La Jolla Valley Walk-in Camp, have online reservations systems where you can check their availability. If you see that not many sites are left for the days you want, move quickly to finalize your plans and make a reservation. Summer and weekends are the most popular times. Musch Trail and La Jolla Valley Walk-in Camp are first-come, first-served campgrounds that must be accessed on foot and, generally, do not fill up.

5) Book travel

If travelling from outside of Los Angeles, the sooner you can book travel, the more money you will save. TCT hikers will need to book ferry tickets. Seats will book up in the summertime, but otherwise there should be availability. Call the ferry companies to figure out how much space is left on the days you are considering.

There may be additional considerations before finalizing any of these steps, such as difficult work schedules or hiking partners with cold feet. The overall planning process can be iterative. Say you take a closer look at the camping options and determine that you want to spend a whole day at one campsite. Now you are adding a day to your estimate of trail days in step 2 above, which alters all following steps. Take a quick glance at the highlights and challenges of the trail and ask whether you might like an extra day somewhere before finalizing any travel.

Micro-Planning

Now that you have a general idea of the pace and schedule of your hike, it is time to take a detailed look at the trail and determine your day-by-day schedule in order to book campsites. There are not a lot of camping options on the TCT and BBT, so the best way to start would be a list of all campsites and then ask yourself if you will be staying at or skipping each one.

Using the camping table from Section 2d as an example along with the elevation profile from the appendix, we can get a feel for what a hike along the TCT would look like each day.

Campground	Distance (mi)	Cumulative (mi)	Elevation (ft)
Hermit Gulch	1.7*	1.7*	262
Blackjack	15.7	15.7	1,512
Little Harbor	7.2	22.9	33
Two Harbors (0.4 mi E)	5.2	28.1	39
Parsons' Landing	6.6	34.7	13
Parsons' Landing (out and back to Starlight Beach)**	9.2	43.9	13
Two Harbors via West End Rd**	7.5	51.4	39

* Via Hermit Gulch Trail alternate out of Avalon
** Parsons' Landing and Two Harbors are listed twice to reflect the return trip from Starlight Beach to Two Harbors, which passes Parsons' Landing again.

Table 9 – Available TCT Camping Options

As an example, here is my thought process for selecting campsites on a westbound TCT hike, starting from Avalon:

For the first campsite, my campground options are Hermit Gulch at 1.7 miles from the ferry, Blackjack at 15.7 miles, and Little Harbor at 22.9 miles. I eliminate Little Harbor because hiking almost 23 miles on the first day while starting from the mainland might be tough. Hermit Gulch and Blackjack are now my only options. The decision is whether to take on the 15.7 miles after a boat ride from the mainland or hang out in Avalon and get an early start from Hermit Gulch the next day. Because there is no time like the present, I decide to go for it and camp at Blackjack the first night.

So now on Day 2, I have 7.2 miles to Little Harbor, 12.4 miles to Two Harbors, or 19 miles to Parsons' Landing from Blackjack. Knowing how beautiful the beach at Little Harbor is, I don't have to think much about this and decide Night 2 will be at Little Harbor.

Day 3 options are a 5.2 mile hike to Two Harbors or 11.8 miles to Parsons' Landing with an option to go out to Starlight Beach and finish the TCT and then return to Parsons' to camp, making 21 miles on the day. Keeping the mileage at 11.8 miles to Parsons' Landing sounds nice. Maybe I will do the 1-mile side trip up to Silver Peak.

For the final day, I am left with 9.2 miles to Starlight Beach and back to Parsons' Landing plus the 7.5-mile West End Road route to Two Harbors to finish the hike – a total of 16.7 miles on that day. With 16.7 miles on my last day, I will be booking the late ferry out of Two Harbors and hopefully have enough time for burgers and beers before getting on the boat. That schedule would look something like this:

Campground	Cumulative (mi)	Day	Distance (mi)
Hermit Gulch	1.7*		
Blackjack	15.7	1	15.7
Little Harbor	22.9	2	7.2
Two Harbors (0.4 mi E)	28.1		
Parsons' Landing	34.7	3	11.8
Parsons' Landing (out and back to Starlight Beach)**	43.9		
Two Harbors via West End Rd**	51.4	4	16.7

Table 10 – Sample Itinerary for 4-Day TCT Hike

There could be many different reasons for selecting a certain mileage for each day. The description above is just an example of the factors that go into narrowing down an itinerary in order to make your camping reservations. In general, the campgrounds are lenient if you decide to change your reservation with enough notice, but if you are hiking during a busy time, other campgrounds could be booked and your options may be limited. The earlier you can make a reservation, the better.

b. Food

The food you bring with you can bring a lot of enjoyment out on the trail. If you are not a good cook, don't worry. Everything tastes better on the trail. Meals should, generally, be simple to prepare, lightweight, non-perishable, and varied. There are some exceptions to this. For example, you can bring perishable foods for your first day on the trail. They likely will be a little heavier than dry, non-perishable food, but you are consuming it the first day before it goes bad, so you won't be burdened by it the whole trip.

Keep it simple

Keeping meals simple will give you more time to hike, relax at camp, and require less time for cleaning up. A great example of this is breakfast. Oatmeal seems to be the go-to breakfast meal for backpacking, but it requires time to heat water and then clean your cooking pot in the morning. Breakfast shakes, pastries, bagels with spreads, or cereal bars are all quick and get you going out of camp.

Prepare as much as possible at home to reduce clean up and time required in camp as well as to minimize cookware carried. If you want to cook gourmet, go for it. Just make sure you remember all equipment required. For example, can openers are an easy one to forget. Also, more complicated meals require more fuel. Water may only take a few minutes to bring to a boil. If your meal requires an additional six minutes of boiling beyond that, you may need to double the amount of fuel you carry. Large groups can cook big, complicated meals without much hassle by sharing cookware and ingredients.

Keep it light

The food you carry can have a lot of weight- and volume-savings if you pay attention. Packaging should be stripped down to reduce bulk. Some foods will have water weight, like canned foods, so if possible, keep these to a minimum or reserve them for just dinners to save weight. Dried fruits are a great way to get a lot of nutritious snacks without all the water weight in fresh fruits. A couple fresh fruits are good for breakfast or a lunch snack, but consider these are heavier than dried snacks.

[i] Generally, plan for 1-2 pounds of food per day. You will develop hiker hunger after a few days, so if your trip is longer, you can plan less food in the beginning and more towards the end.

Keep it fun

Variety is important while hiking. You may think you love peanut butter and plan on putting it on everything until you actually put it on everything and then can't even look at it anymore. Different meals give you something to look forward to. As your tastes change throughout the day and trip, you will want a few options to turn to for quick lift. Eating the same food every day takes the excitement and motivation out of stopping for lunch or a snack.

When you have the time to plan and prepare meals ahead of your trip, it can make a huge difference. Dehydrating your own food takes a lot of preparation time and forethought but will bring home-cooked meals and flavors on the trail. They also are easy to prepare. You just add boiling water to rehydrate. Trail foods can be bland. Bring extra seasoning or sauces to enhance your meals for little weight cost.

Carbohydrates are important for sustained energy. Protein helps build and recover muscle. Salts and electrolytes must be replaced throughout the day as you sweat on long climbs. Consider these nutritional components as well as vitamins and minerals when assembling your meal plan.

You will be drinking tap water for these hikes, which is not always as fresh tasting as water from a natural source. Powdered drink mixes are great for when you get sick of the taste of water or want something sweet with a meal.

Meal Planning

At almost two pounds per day, food can add a lot of weight to your pack, so try and be realistic about how much you will be eating for each meal. It's easy to get carried away in the grocery store before a hike, but, unless you already have a huge appetite from working out a lot, your hunger won't kick in on the first day. Lay out each day's food in front of you in a pile and ask whether, on a normal day, you could eat everything or if it looks like a challenge. Then adjust accordingly.

Another strategy to avoid carrying extra food is to count the exact number of meals you will eat over the course of the hike. Create a grid with the number of days you will be hiking as columns and the meals as rows. Mark the meals you need to carry each day. Usually, the first day you will eat a meal at home or on the way to the trail, in which case you would not have to pack a breakfast or lunch. Same with the last day on the trail. Depending on your anticipated finish time, you may not need a lunch and likely not need a dinner. If you plan to grab a meal on the trail (for example the grills at Airport in the Sky or Two Harbors on the TCT or one of the restaurants in Topanga on the BBT), then you could choose not to include a lunch that day. Rather than simply bringing one of every meal for each trail day, you can whittle down the exact meals needed and save yourself a few pounds.

Example:

Meal	Day 1	Day 2	Day 3	Total
Breakfast		x	x	2
Lunch	x	x		2
Snack	x	x	x	3
Dinner	x	x		2

Table 11 – Sample 3-Day Meal Plan

From the table above, I need 2 breakfasts, 2 lunches, 3 snacks, and 2 dinners to cover three days and two nights on the trail. No breakfast on Day 1, that will be on the way to the trail or at home, and an early finish on Day 3 means I don't need a lunch or dinner. So for a three-day hike, you only need about two days' worth of every meal, plus some extra snacks.

c. Resupply

Both trails covered in this book are short enough to not require resupply. However, there are some options for resupply that could lighten your pack from the start of your hike.

Trans-Catalina Trail

There are three locations where resupply is possible along the trail: Avalon, Airport in the Sky, and Two Harbors:

Avalon

Avalon has full food resupply at the two grocery stores in town and many camp fuel options at the hardware store. Unfortunately, these will be located either at the very start or end of the hike so will not allow you to carry less food along the way. Instead, Avalon is a good safety net if you forget something at home and need to pick it up before the start of your hike or if you are completely out of food at the end of your hike. The Vons Express has the best options for groceries while Chet's Hardware has camp fuel including isobutane/propane canisters and denatured alcohol in containers as small as 16 ounces.

Airport in the Sky

Airport in the Sky has a grill with burgers and sandwiches that could substitute one meal in your pack. Keep in mind the airport is only 2 miles from Blackjack Campground, so depending on your day, you may not feel like burgers first thing in the morning. They also have some small bags of chips, drinks, and candy available.

Two Harbors

Two Harbors has good resupply options at the general store as well as a restaurant. You could replace a meal from your pack with one at the restaurant and carry less food at the start of your trip, knowing you will have the option of picking up more food at the general store if you run low. You could carry only enough food to get you to the general store and then resupply the rest of the trip from there. They carry isobutane/propane canisters as well as liquid white gas (not for alcohol stoves!) but not denatured alcohol or Heet®.

[i] The best option for resupply on the TCT is to probably err on the side of carrying less food to make your pack lighter for the first couple of days and then reevaluate your food supplies at the Two Harbors general store.

Backbone Trail

There is only one convenient place to resupply on the BBT, and it requires a somewhat dangerous roadwalk on windy roads with narrow shoulders. The town of Topanga lies only 0.5 miles from the trail at two locations. You could walk into town on either Topanga Canyon Boulevard/Highway 27 at mile 12 or Old Topanga Canyon Road at mile 12.8, and then walk back out of town on the other road to avoid fully backtracking. There are several restaurants, a bar, and a general store in this small mountain community at the intersection of Old Topanga Canyon Road and Topanga Canyon Boulevard. There is also a library and post office all within walking distance. The proximity to the eastern terminus makes this not an ideal location for a resupply point, but it could be just right for a meal in town.

Caching

Caching food and water on the Backbone Trail may be the better option. There are many road crossings along the route, and the long stretch of trail without water between Circle X Ranch and Malibu Creek State Park would be the perfect place to leave a water cache. Make sure your cache is concealed well so someone does not take it or throw it out, leaving you with nothing. Do not disturb the environment when leaving your cache and pack out all trash. Respect private property and do not store caches on private property near the trail. Crossings at Latigo Canyon Road (mile

33.1), Kanan Dume Road (mile 35.4), Encinal Canyon Road (mile 40.3), Mulholland Highway (mile 41.5), or Yerba Buena Road (mile 45.9) would be good locations for a water cache between Circle X Ranch and Malibu Creek State Park and could also help avoid walking several miles off trail to Circle X Ranch for water. When contacted, the California State Parks did not have an issue with caching as long as the environment is not disturbed and the cache is not abandoned, but the National Park Service is opposed to caching, so cache at your own risk.

d. Training

Backpacking requires both mental and physical strength, but finishing a thru-hike is mainly mental. It takes a lot more than being physically fit and having all the best gear. You still need to put down miles and push through obstacles along the way. However, being in good physical shape will make the mental portion easier. The following section discusses some of what it takes from both your mind and body to complete a thru-hike.

Mental Preparation

There is a popular thru-hiking phrase to describe motivation that goes "it's not about the destination, it's about the journey". The views at the starting and ending trailheads may not stand out in your memories of the trip, but everything that you had to go through to get there will.

Your journey will be full of tests. You must accept and expect this before heading out. Your journey will not be easy. You will sweat. Your feet will hurt. Your shoulders and hips will become sore or even bruised from the weight of your pack. You will probably get lost. Any one of these tests is an opportunity to turn around and end the trip or to discover what your mental toughness amounts to. Those who make it to their "destination" are those who can enjoy the journey and understand that every roadblock along the way is just part of the experience. The destination is best used as a motivating force and a vessel to create memories and experiences forged through overcoming situations you never fully understood until you faced them. Have confidence in your own abilities and keep walking forward.

Forget the end of the trail is even there. It will come upon you on its own. Set smaller goals you can meet throughout the day and appreciate these moments and victories as you achieve them. Focus on your next water source, climb, or campsite, and you can distract yourself enough from thinking about the impossibly far off "destination".

Physical Preparation

Walking for days through the mountains with the weight of your pack resting on your shoulders can lead to a variety of physical ailments, many occurring at the same time. Your preparation should focus on minimizing these incidents of pain on the trail. This involves not only strengthening your muscles but hardening your feet, adjusting to heat, and familiarizing yourself with your gear.

Backpacking requires strength and endurance. Focus on improving leg strength through walking or running inclines, lunges, and squats. A low-impact option for leg strengthening and injury prevention are resistance band exercises similar to those for rehabbing knee or hip injuries. These exercises can isolate specific muscles and tendons as well as strengthen knees, calves, ankles, and quadriceps with less risk for injury compared to running or weight training.

Running is an excellent activity for building cardiovascular fitness and translates very well to backpacking. If you can already run long distances, you may find backpacking comes easy to you. A good measure of fitness for these hikes would be to run three miles, at any pace, without stopping. You may find you don't need much training at all, depending on how difficult a three-mile run is for you. If you can run six miles in one exercise session, regardless of stopping for breaks, you should be in great shape for backpacking. Try and throw in a few hills on your running routes.

Staying on your feet is another physical challenge. Walking all day plus the added weight of your pack will leave your feet sore and weary. Prior to your trip, you can take steps to acclimate your feet to these conditions and make easier and more miles on the trail. Spend time walking or running on trails as much as possible, ideally using the footwear you will wear on the hike. Try not to rest for at least half an hour or longer, and learn the limits of your feet. Running is a great training activity, because it not only helps build strength and stamina, but also toughens your feet. Spending time in your hiking shoes will further help break in any hard edges that could cause blisters later on. Try walking at least 10 miles on a one-day hike in advance of your trip.

If you will be switching to lightweight footwear from heavier footwear, you may experience soreness of stabilizer muscles around your feet, ankles, and lower legs. It is best to slowly strengthen these muscles over several weeks than on the first day of a five-day hike. Walk or run on uneven trail as much as possible to work all stabilizer muscles.

6. Gear

Backpacking gear is an important component to completing and enjoying your journey. There are so many options to choose from that the gear selection process can take longer than hiking the trail sometimes. In this section, I will discuss essential items for the trails and compare the most appropriate styles for the TCT and BBT. Deciding on a style will quickly narrow down your choices to a few models made in that style, allowing you to easily compare criteria, such as weight, functionality, and price, to make a decision. The TCT and BBT are in the same climate and neither of them requires specialized or technical gear, so the recommendations given would apply for both trails.

a. Clothing

Your clothing setup from colder environments will no longer apply for Southern California conditions. Your warmest layers may only be worn at night, if at all. You are also less likely to experience sustained rain that could require redundant layers. These conditions allow you to carry only a few select clothing items and save weight and space in your pack.

Hiking Clothes

Your main concern during the daytime will be shielding yourself from the sun while staying comfortable enough to exert yourself. Covering yourself head-to-toe solves one problem, but depending on the clothing, may only increase your body temperature and effort required to cover miles. People respond to sun exposure differently, so if you know you have especially sensitive skin, definitely err on the side of caution when selecting clothing to protect you.

Two strategies to handle this dual threat are to cover exposed skin in loose, breathable fabrics or to wear shorts and a T-shirt while constantly applying sunblock to exposed areas. You will need to apply sunblock no matter your clothing setup, but will need to cover a larger area and use more if wearing shorts and a T-shirt. You will not need to protect your legs from overgrown trails unless you plan on doing some bushwhacking. Sun would be the primary reason for covering up. Another option is to use a hiking-specific umbrella, which is discussed further at the end of this chapter in Section 6g *Other Essentials*.

Shirt

You will be very familiar with your shirt by the end of the trip. It spends the most time on your body, and the comfort levels have a great effect on your experience. A popular choice for sun-exposed hiking conditions is a long-sleeved shirt with buttons or zippers that can be opened to increase air circulation to your core. I primarily wore a button-up shirt with vents on the back and armpit as well as buttoned sleeve cuffs, which stayed open while hiking and could be rolled up in shady sections for more air circulation. If you shop around for hiking-specific sun protection shirts, they all seem to be some shade of beige that does not absorb light and looks fine if it gets dirty, but they are not the most stylish. Any shirt would provide protection as long as it blocks light from reaching your skin, so don't hesitate to stray from the taupe department.

Another great option is simply a comfortable, breathable, moisture-wicking T-shirt if combined with a liberal application of sunblock. You probably already have one you like hiking or running in. Avoid black or dark colors, which absorb sunlight. You will be sweating a lot, and your shirt should dry fast in the sun. When I arrive at a breaking point, I set my shirt out in the sun, and it will dry by the time I'm ready to start hiking again.

Pants

You can usually find the beige hiking-specific sun protection pants right next to the shirts. They work the same way, providing cover from the sun in a light-reflecting fabric that can breathe through adjustments like zippers and vents. I find pants to be restrictive when hiking no matter how many zippers they have, so I prefer running or basketball shorts with sun block on the exposed portion of my legs. Basketball shorts are a little longer than running shorts so provide more sun protection, but you may also find them restrictive when compared to running shorts. Pockets should be available no matter the style of pants you choose and are great for storing items like maps that need to be accessed quickly. If you have always hiked in pants, I understand the aversion to change from something you are comfortable with but don't knock shorts until you've tried them.

Face and Neck Protection

A hat serves three main purposes. Get the sun out of your eyes, prevent sweat from running down your face, and, most importantly, prevent sunburn on your face and neck. There are many styles of wide-brimmed hats that can protect all of your face and neck from the sun. A ball cap is a comfortable and convenient option but does not fully cover your neck. Either apply a lot of sunblock regularly or wear a bandana underneath the hat so it hangs down and covers your neck during sunny sections. There are ball caps specifically for sun-intense hiking or running that have hanging fabric attachments for more protection. With so many options, you surely will find something both functional and stylish.

Camp Clothes

When temperatures are low at the end of the day and in the morning, you will want a change of warmer clothes. You won't need an exceptional amount of insulating clothes, since overnight lows may never drop below 50°F in the summertime and rarely below freezing all year. Check the forecast beforehand to be sure. Temperature forecasts should be stable as well as precipitation forecasts, although you are only likely to see rain in the winter and early spring.

You probably won't need more than one pair of warm clothes. They will mostly be worn just at night and not while hiking, so should stay somewhat clean. Additionally, because sustained rain is rare, you're not at much risk for warm clothes getting wet and needing an extra pair. At the very least, bring a pair of thermal top and bottoms (aka long johns). They are comfortable, can be the first part of a layering system, and also can be worn while hiking to get you going on cold mornings. On my TCT hike in early October, even my thermal layers stayed packed away the entire trip.

You could get away with a set of thermal top and bottoms and no other warm clothes if you are hiking in the summer but otherwise will want a jacket, too. Down jackets are preferred, since they are the lightest and usually warmest option but can be expensive. Down also does not function if it gets wet, since it requires the loft of down feathers to create air pockets and insulate your body heat. A light fleece would work well for these trails in place of a down jacket but likely will be bulkier and heavier.

A warm hat for nighttime is a great comfort if temps do get lower than expected and a good safety factor with little weight cost. Sleeping socks, which you only wear in your tent not while hiking, fall into that same role. If you are hiking in winter, they may still not be 100% necessary but very comfortable and a buffer against unexpected cold weather.

Additional Clothing

A rain jacket is a necessary item that may never be used on these trails. If you are hiking in the summertime, or even late spring and early fall, there is very little chance you will experience rain. Maybe you can use it as a pillow. Unfortunately, if you don't pack a rain jacket, its absence actually will cause rain, somehow, by altering weather patterns. This is a scientific fact. If you wanted to taunt the hiking gods and leave it at home, you would probably still survive. Look for rain shells that simply have a single waterproof layer with no extra netting or jacket layers inside.

Gloves are not necessary for warmth on these trails. There are special gloves to prevent sunburn on your hands that some people prefer in particularly sunny conditions like these trails, but those would be an optional item. Fleece or down pants are an option if you are hiking in the winter or the forecast is calling for colder temps overnight. They are probably overkill most of the year though.

Washing Clothes

The hot, dry, and sandy conditions on the TCT and BBT will no doubt leave your socks full of fine sand. Keep your feet happy by rinsing your socks frequently (be considerate of those around you), then hang them on the outside of your pack and let them dry as you hike. It won't take long for the sun to dry them out. Rotate your socks frequently and clean your feet, too, either at a water source or with a wet wipe to maintain good hygiene and avoid various foot issues.

Your best bet for washing clothes will probably be at the piped water sources available along both trails. Be considerate that Southern California is in a prolonged drought and that resources, particularly on Catalina Island, are scarce. Don't use more than you need and be considerate of others using the water source. Wash clothing at least 200 feet away from natural water sources. Use biodegradable soap, if any. There are laundry machines next to the bathrooms in Two Harbors on Catalina Island.

Sample Clothing List

Worn Items

- Long-sleeved breathable/vented hiking shirt
- Shorts
- Socks
- Baseball hat
- Bandana for shade

Carried Items

- Down jacket
- Thermal top and bottoms
- Rain jacket
- Wool hat
- Extra socks

b. Hiking

Basic hiking gear usually consists of footwear, a backpack, and optional trekking poles. The physical act of transporting your body and gear across a mountain range is most directly impacted by these items. Your comfort level while hiking greatly depends on them.

Footwear

Generally, there are three categories of footwear for backpacking: hiking boots, hiking shoes, and trail runners. Hiking boots are the traditional footwear of backpackers and provide total protection for your foot, but they are the heaviest and most expensive of these three. Hiking shoes are an in-between for boots and trail runners and provide much of the protection of boots without the weight and bulk. Trail runners are the lightest option and provide agility, flexibility, and breathability that boots or hiking shoes cannot. Lighter footwear does not require the same amount of breaking in that boots do. You should still test out your footwear for a few miles before setting out on a multi-day trip. But in general, the lighter the shoe the gentler it is on your foot.

| Hiking Boot | Hiking Shoe | Trail Runner |

Figure 31 – Typical Hiking Footwear Options

I would recommend wearing a light hiking shoe or, preferably, trail runner if you have experience with lighter footwear. Less weight on your feet means less work for every step you take along the trail. The trails are not rugged enough to necessitate tougher footwear, like a heavy boot, to stabilize and protect your feet over rough, rocky trail. A lighter shoe will also breathe much better than a boot, which you will appreciate on the hot, sun-exposed climbs found on these trails. One very important caveat is that if you are carrying a very heavy pack, you may require heavier footwear, such as a hiking shoe or boot, to support the additional weight. Look for thick soles regardless of the type of footwear you choose. Some trail runners are not meant to be used when carrying weight such as a pack. A thicker sole will help deal with the additional weight.

The most important factor when selecting a shoe is a comfortable fit. Seems obvious, but it is easy to get caught up in a brand or style of shoe that someone else recommended for you. Some brands run very narrow, others wide, and everyone's foot is shaped different. Don't get married to the idea of a specific shoe until you have tried it on and can be sure that there are no tight spots or pressure points on your feet from the shoe that could create blisters after a few miles. Try several different brands and models before buying anything and go out for some trial hikes or walks around your neighborhood, with and without a pack, to ensure the fit is good before setting out for your trip. If you start developing hot spots or blisters, consider another shoe.

My Choice: When hiking these trails, I wore a Brooks Cascadia 8 and an Altra Lone Peak 2.0. Both are lightweight trail runners that have reasonably thick soles and good breathability. Additionally, I have very wide feet and the Lone Peak has an oversized toe box. Thus, my feet are not cramped, I don't have to break in the shoes at all, and I have never had blisters. Personally, I prefer the Lone Peak for the wider fit, but the Cascadia is also an excellent shoe for lightweight backpacking. Just don't get the Cascadia 10. There was a serious design flaw with that model that caused tearing across the toe box after only 100 miles or so.

Trail runners also cost much less than boots, often less than half the price of boots. A boot will last much longer, but you would have to hike 1,500 to 2,000 miles in a pair of boots before breaking even versus a trail runner. Another way to save money is to identify a model of a shoe that you like, then search online for the previous year's version. The older models are just as good and can be half the price.

When deciding between different models, a few things to look for, besides the perfect fit, are the tread, sole thickness, and toe protection offered by the shoe. These will all be immediately apparent from a quick glance and can help eliminate or distinguish models. The tread refers to the outsole, or bottom of the shoe, that will interface with the ground. You want something that will grip the surface and provide stability on steep grades. Sole thickness is important to provide cushioning from the weight of your body and pack while standing all day. Trail runners not designed for backpacking can have very thin soles. Toe protection is not as important on these trails but lighter footwear may neglect to include any hard layer around the front of the shoe to help with bumping your feet against rocks and roots.

Insoles

Most shoes do not come out of the box with robust insoles. If you are having issues with soreness or feel your shoe's insole is irritating your foot, consider buying new insoles. Feel free to look outside of hiking-specific insoles. Work boot insoles are meant to support a lot of weight all day and will provide some extra cushioning, especially if your shoe has a thin sole. Cut the insoles to the fit of your shoe. Consider that a thicker insole will make the fit of your footwear tighter.

Waterproofing

Waterproofing your footwear is not necessary on these trails. You will rarely, if at all, encounter streams or water. Waterproofing reduces the breathability of your footwear and will make your feet hotter and sweat more.

Gaiters

Light gaiters may be a good choice for these trails to prevent dirt and rocks from entering your shoe. One downside of lighter footwear is that they generally have lower collars, which allow debris to more easily enter the shoe. Gaiters will cut down on all those little rocks and sticks that get into your shoe and scream for you to stop hiking and tend to them. However, gaiters also reduce breathability and increase the temperature of your foot and legs so go with the smallest possible gaiter. Gaiters that cover your full leg are not necessary and more appropriate for serious bushwhacking or snow travel.

Camp Shoes

Lightweight sandals or flip-flops would be a great addition if you will be staying at any of the beaches on the TCT. Camp shoes are an optional item for both trails that can give you a little relief at the end of the day if you are having foot problems.

Backpacks

Your backpack should, ideally, be the last item purchased. The backpack you use will mostly depend on the volume of your other gear. Due to favorable weather on these trails, you should be going with a light setup that can accommodate a smaller and lighter backpack.

Backpack volume is usually measured in liters. 50 liters is a good starting point for shopping around. To get a better idea of the difference between a 40- and 70-liter pack, visit an outdoor retailer and browse the backpack section. Usually the smaller the volume, the lighter the pack, but some lightweight packs may have smaller frames and supports that reduce weight without losing volume.

Features like hip belt pockets, water bottle pockets that are accessible while hiking, outer mesh pockets for quick storage, and overall organization of the pack are factors to look for when selecting a pack. Personal hiking style and preferences will determine the factors that end up taking priority.

Most retail stores only carry internal frame packs, which have a rigid support system, usually hard plastic, mounted to the padding at your back. These packs are more comfortable and can shoulder higher volumes and weight when compared to ultralight packs. They usually also have more organizational bells and whistles. They can weigh twice as much as ultralight packs. They are usually more expensive but, depending on your use, can last a lifetime.

Ultralight packs save weight by using sleeping pads in place of a rigid internal frame support. Generally, they can't carry as much weight and volume as a traditional pack and are less durable. However, they will still last a significant amount of time if you are just hiking a few weekend and multi-day trips per year. They require thoughtful packing, due to the lack of a rigid frame, to ensure items do not bulge awkwardly into your back. Their main advantage is that you will be carrying one to two pounds less weight over the course of your trip compared to a traditional pack. Ultralight packs are typically only available online.

My Choice: I used a frameless pack that makes use of my sleeping pad as the main structural support and has huge mesh outer pockets with one main body pocket. This frame system makes the pack much lighter and saves volume, since my sleeping pad is stored as the frame. But it also requires careful packing. I like this pack because of how lightweight and simple it is. While the mesh side pockets are great for keeping items accessible, only having one main body pocket makes organization and access to items difficult.

Rain Protection

Two strategies for protection against rain include internal or external waterproof membranes. An external system would be a plastic bag fit around the outside of your pack with holes for straps and hip belts cut out or a manufactured pack rain cover. An internal system uses plastic bags to pack up all your items inside the pack and disregards the outside of the pack. The internal system ensures that your important items are sealed away while the external system could allow exposure to rain where the membrane must open to allow shoulder straps and hip belts to pass through.

You are not likely to have huge issues with rain on this trail, but it is good to be prepared just in case. Carrying a durable trash bag in your pack that you can pull out if it ever rains is the simplest measure.

Trekking Poles

Trekking poles are a non-essential item that could help in many ways. Primarily, they assist while walking and improve climbing, descending, and overall balance. Additionally, some shelter designs make use of trekking poles for support, allowing you to save the weight of tent poles.

Generally, trekking poles decrease stress on your knees during descents. Both trails have sustained descents, so if you have a history of knee problems, consider trekking poles. They also work to create a rhythm to your walking and assist with balance when rock hopping.

Most trekking poles are divided in sections and collapsible to allow for storage and height adjustments, which is helpful, for example, if they are being used for shelter supports. The sections are secured with either a twist lock or a clasp lock at the joints. The twist locks can be cumbersome and prone to breaking. Clasp locks are much easier to operate, repair, and are generally more reliable, but also slightly more expensive. A cheap alternative to buying hiking-specific trekking poles is to repurpose old ski poles or use a walking stick. This option doesn't work if you need adjustable hiking poles for your shelter.

[i] While trekking poles are not essential, but I would highly recommend them for the TCT. Certain sections of the trail are ridiculously steep on flat dirt roads with not much relief for footholds. The trekking poles provide you with some assistance on these sections.

c. Sleep System

After a long day of mashing miles, you need to spend some time recovering for the next day's hike. Your sleep system is made up of a combination of gear items that not only protect you from the elements, but also allow you to recharge and tackle tomorrow's challenge. Your sleep system is very important for this reason, but also likely includes the heaviest items you will carry. Extra comfort at night means extra work during the day to haul that gear around. Choose your sleep system carefully and consider whether certain comforts you think you can't live without really are essential.

Shelters

Depending on your current shelter, there is a tremendous opportunity to achieve weight savings on the TCT and BBT by switching to a lightweight system. You should not experience bugs or difficult weather conditions, which are the primary reasons for armoring yourself with a robust shelter. That said, lighter shelters require a little more work to set up. So if you are not good with getting a taut pitch for a tarp, or other tension-line shelters, practice a little bit before heading out. It only takes one night in the rain to learn how to set them up the right way.

Freestanding

Tarp Tent

Bivy

Tarp

Figure 32 – Typical Hiking Shelter Options

Freestanding

These are the traditional backpacking tent with poles, a rain fly, and inner net. They are the easiest to set up, offer the most protection, and generally are more comfortable. They get their name because they do not require stakes or tension lines for their support so are standing freely. They can weigh several times the weight of lightweight shelters and offer almost too much protection for the TCT and BBT. If you currently have a freestanding shelter, switching to a lightweight tarp or tarp tent could save you a few pounds. Freestanding shelters work great for couples or anyone sharing a shelter, since you can split the weight up between two people, although that strategy would also apply for any shelter.

Tarp Tent

A tarp tent is a much lighter option than a freestanding shelter with much of the same protection. Tension lines provide the shelter's structure with one or two small support poles that usually can be substituted by adjustable trekking poles. Additionally, tarp tents only have one wall, the outer tarp, rather than separate walls for bug and rain protection. If you are not totally comfortable sleeping exposed to the elements, tarp tents are fully enclosed and will provide you with a lot of the same comforts of a freestanding tent while drastically reducing your pack weight.

Tarp tents require practice setting up. If you do not have experience with using tension lines to achieve a taut pitch, give it a couple of tries in your backyard or spend one night in the woods with it before hitting the trail.

Tarp

A tarp is a very simple shelter that saves the weight of a floor, zippers, bug netting, vestibules, and possibly tent poles if you carry adjustable trekking poles. They usually weigh less than a pound, and if you use lightweight fabrics, like cuben fiber, your shelter may weigh as little as half a pound. Some people are not comfortable sleeping unless fully enclosed by a shelter, but the TCT and BBT are a perfect opportunity to step outside of your comfort zone with little risk. Even though the back, front, and some of the sides are completely open, you do get great protection from the rain. I carried a basic catenary cut tarp for almost 3,000 miles on the Continental Divide Trail through some awful weather at high elevations and did not have any problems with rain getting in.

Like a tarp tent, it requires tension lines to set up so get some practice before taking it out on the trail. Another great benefit of a tarp is that it can be set up in many ways. You can raise the sides and tie them off up high to more easily enter the shelter or get them down tight to the ground for rain protection. They can also be easily deployed in the daytime to provide shade for a lunch break or shelter from rain.

There are two main types of tarps. A catenary cut tarp has a curved ridgeline and tapers down the sides, so it's wider in the front. It allows for tighter pitches, but there are less options for different setups. A flat tarp is cut like a rectangle and can be set up in many ways, depending on your tarp skills, but it may be more difficult to get a taut pitch. Regardless of the style of the tarp, it must be paired with a ground sheet, since it does not have a floor.

Cowboy Camping

There is no lighter or faster setup than taking out your groundsheet and lying on top of it. You can cowboy camp no matter what shelter you have. If you are planning on doing it extensively, carrying a robust shelter will be a little wasteful. I like to cowboy camp primarily and have a tarp as backup in case of inclement weather. I was able to cowboy camp every night on the BBT, and I might have missed a close look at a bobcat had I been in a tent. Cowboy camping saves a lot of time at camp and gets you going in the morning faster since you don't have to break down a shelter or lay there contemplating whether you are going to get out of your shelter or not.

Bivy

A bivy is simply a membrane over your sleeping bag and body to protect you from the bugs and elements. They are extremely confining but also lightweight. If your forecast shows five days of sunshine and you plan on cowboy camping, a bivy could provide some extra protection with little weight cost, depending on the style of bivy.

Hammock

I would not recommend a hammock for either trail, but especially the TCT. There are not enough trees around, and even if your campground has trees, you can't guarantee that the specific site you reserved will have trees arranged in a way to accommodate a hammock. Parsons' Landing is on the beach, so it would be impossible to hammock there.

Groundsheet

If you will be using a tarp, a ground sheet is necessary to protect you and your gear from getting dirty or wet if it has recently rained. A groundsheet is not necessary if you have a fully-enclosed shelter, but be careful with your site selection and clear rocks, sticks, or anything else that may puncture your shelter floor.

Tyvek® is a very durable and waterproof material commonly used as a groundsheet. It is cheap, easy to pack up, and will not rip. Plastic membranes are a lighter option for a groundsheet but are not nearly as durable as Tyvek® and can trap condensation underneath them, so that everything on the ground sticks to it when you pack up in the morning. If you are careful with handling your groundsheet and site selection, a plastic groundsheet will work fine at a fraction of the weight of store-bought groundsheets. Common plastic materials used are painter drop cloths (around 3mm thickness) or a material called polyolefin used for window insulation. Painter drop cloths will be more durable but slightly heavier. A polyolefin groundsheet could weigh as little as two ounces. Whether you choose plastic or Tyvek®, both found at hardware stores, you can have a ground sheet for just a few bucks.

My Choice: I would recommend planning on cowboy camping on a groundsheet for these trails and carrying a tarp in case of bad weather. The tarp may be more useful to get shade during the daytime. If you are not comfortable sleeping out in the elements, then a tarp tent is a great lightweight option. Whatever shelter you take, make sure it is seam-sealed.

Look on the inside of the shelter up at the seams where a needle has drawn thread through the shelter membrane and created a hole. If you don't see a layer of coating over the seams, then it is not seam-sealed. You could also wait until it rains to find out quickly whether it is seam-sealed or not.

Sleeping Bags/Quilts

For these trails, you can get away with a high temperature rating sleeping bag or quilt, which will give you some weight savings compared to more robust sleeping bags. A rating of 40 degrees is a good starting place. If you are buying a sleeping bag you intend to use on other hikes, go with a lower rating, since most hikes will not have conditions this friendly. If you are hiking in the summer, you can go with an even higher temperature rating.

Sleeping bag or quilt insulation will either be a synthetic material or down. Synthetic retains its warming properties when wet but is heavier. Down is lighter and more compressible but does not perform as well when wet. You are not at much risk for rain, so a down sleeping bag or quilt is recommended.

Side Note on Quilts: Down insulation only works when there is loft in the bag from the down feathers creating pockets of air. When those pockets of air are compressed, either from being wet or because you are lying on top of them, they are not providing insulation. The theory behind quilts is that the material you are lying on top of is not functioning, so it is essentially dead weight. A quilt eliminates the weight of that material plus the zipper so will be lighter than an equivalent temperature rating sleeping bag. Additionally, you are not confined to a zipped up sleeping bag while sleeping and can more easily move around in your sleep or get air circulation if you are too hot. These trails would be an excellent time to experiment with quilts. Quilts are also one of the easiest pieces of gear to make yourself.

Sleeping Pads

Depending on the person, a sleeping pad can be the most crucial item carried. Without a good night's sleep, you will have a tough time making miles the next day. Sleeping with the hard ground against your hips and knees all night can be very painful. Only you can be the judge of how you will be affected by these things. Experiencing sleeping on the ground is the best way to find your limits. There are two main categories of sleeping pads, inflatable pads and closed-cell foam pads.

R-value is a measurement of the insulating properties of the sleeping pad. It is not important to know what exactly the number means, just that higher numbers mean more insulation and thus a warmer pad. R-value does not have anything to do with how comfortable the pad will be, but comfort does correlate, roughly, with the R-value. Compare R-values between sleeping pads to help make a decision when buying, but keep in mind that warmth is not a major factor for these trails, so lower R-values will probably be acceptable.

Inflatable Pads

If you know that a good mattress will be essential for a solid rest at night, then go with an inflatable sleeping pad. They are heavier and take time and energy to inflate, but you rarely hear people complain about that if it means a good sleep. Adjust the firmness of an inflatable pad by opening the valve while lying on it. Inflatable pads are not only the most comfortable sleeping pad, but also the most compact and warmest available.

Drawbacks of inflatable pads include higher cost and weight, risk of puncture (and therefore not recommended for lunch breaks and use without a groundsheet), and, depending on your shelter, they can slip around on a tent floor. Some inflatable sleeping pads are self-inflating and have a foam layer inside that expands and draws in air when the air valve is opened. These are slightly heavier and less compact but will provide some padding if punctured on the trail and deflated.

Closed-Cell Foam Pads

Foam pads are the light and cheap option for sleeping pads. They are also more durable than inflatable pads and don't have any risk of puncture. They do not compress at all and are usually rolled or folded for storage.

My Choice: I sleep like a rock on any surface after a full day of hiking. Comfort is not as important to me as functionality and weight, so I use a closed-cell foam sleeping pad. A foam pad will not fail, can be deployed for daytime breaks and naps, and is both light and cheap. Additionally, my foam pad is integrated with my pack as the framing support.

d. Food & Water

This section focuses on the various gear items needed to store, prepare, and consume food as well as to store and manage water.

Food Storage

There are no food storage requirements on these trails. However, it is always smart to keep your food and any scented items together, outside of your pack when sleeping, so that small critters don't eat through your gear to get at any food.

On the BBT, I did not have any issues with animals going after my food but both times on the TCT, at Blackjack Campground, I had Catalina foxes try and get my food while my back was turned. I have also had seagulls poach unattended food at the beaches on the TCT and heard from others that they had trouble with squirrels at a couple of campsites. Take advantage of the lockers available at most campgrounds on the TCT and store all your food and scented items in them. You can place your items in any unlocked locker that is available. In the case of Little Harbor, where there were no lockers, I hung my pack and food from the shade structure at our campsite.

Stove & Fuel

There are no considerations for altitude or temperature on these trails that would require specialized cooking equipment. Keep your system simple and light to save time and weight. Most backpacking meals only require heating water, so a complicated stove is not necessary. However, if you know you will be cooking more complex meals, bring an appropriate stove system.

Canister Stoves

Canister stoves are the simplest system to use and cook the fastest. They are comprised of a fuel canister attached to a burner unit that controls the release of pressurized fuel and interfaces with your cookware. The flame is easily extinguished and very controllable. Canister stoves end up weighing slightly more than alcohol systems but are extremely convenient and fast.

Alcohol Stoves

Alcohol stove systems use an open flame from ignited liquid fuel, such as denatured alcohol, to cook meals and heat water. The system works by pouring liquid fuel into a container and setting it on fire. Alcohol stoves cannot be controlled and are difficult to extinguish. When you pour fuel into the stove, all of it must be consumed before the flame is extinguished. They are known for being extremely cheap and lightweight and usually are paired with a windscreen and supports for cookware. It is possible to set your cookware on top of an alcohol stove without a windscreen or support, it just won't be as efficient. Most alcohol stove systems are homemade from aluminum cans and metal flashing. The internet has a wide range of homemade designs that maximize efficiency and minimize weight. You can make your own system with a can and a hole punch, but there are also well-made systems available for purchase that integrate the stove, cookware, supports, and windscreen into one unit.

Stoveless Cooking

An extreme lightweight practice is to go "stoveless". Stoveless cooking involves rehydrating meals in water without any heat source. Most dehydrated meals will do this after sitting in cold water for 30 minutes without a heat source. This system saves the weight of a stove, fuel, and possibly cookware, which can add up to a pound or two. Since dinner is usually the only meal a stove is used for, the thinking is that carrying two pounds of gear for only one meal is not worth the weight. Usually a plastic container with a screw lid is used for rehydrating food to save weight over metal cookware.

My Choice: I would recommend an alcohol stove or canister stove system for these trails. Both systems are very simple and the temperatures are not going to be low enough or the altitudes high enough to affect the cooking system. These trails would also be a good chance to experiment with stoveless cooking, since the temperatures rarely reach below freezing. In my experience with stoveless cooking, you quickly abandon it when the temperature gets close to freezing.

If you are travelling by plane and can't bring denatured alcohol fuel with you, a cheap and commonly found alternative is Heet®, Gas-Line Antifreeze and Water Remover. It works the same as denatured alcohol, costs just a few dollars, and is available at most gas stations. Buy the yellow bottle, not the red one, which will clog up your stove. One bottle is 12 ounces and could last five days, depending on your use. Occasionally, the bottle will not properly reseal, so consider transferring it to another lightweight container.

Bring a redundant flame source, usually a lighter and set of matches. Keep the matches in a dry, safe, never-to-be-used-except-in-case-of-emergency place and primarily use the lighter. If that breaks down somehow, you will have a book of dry matches ready.

[!] Consider your surroundings when cooking, especially with denatured alcohol. Southern California can be extremely dry and subject to wildfires. Denatured alcohol stoves are not easily controlled or extinguished.

Cook on an area of barren ground where no grasses are nearby. Pay attention to your stove and cookware while it is cooking to make sure nothing around it has caught on fire. Be very delicate when handling your food so as not to knock the stove over and spill flaming liquid fuel out onto the volatile grasses found throughout these trails.

Fuel Calculation

Your fuel calculations will depend on the type of meals you have planned for the hike. Typically, fuel will only be used for your dinners, usually boiling two cups of water, but if you will be simmering food for several minutes or drinking coffee or tea, you will need a little bit more fuel for the trip.

Roughly two ounces of denatured alcohol fuel will cook a single backpacking meal requiring two cups of water, although efficient alcohol stove systems could have better results. Conservatively, assume two ounces of fuel for every night on the trail. Add a few more ounces if you will be having coffee every morning or simmering any meals for a long time. 16 ounces of denatured alcohol should be more than enough for a five-day trip. If you are using a canister fuel system, one full four-ounce canister should safely last five days for two people, including coffee every morning.

These fuel calculations are rough estimates and depend on factors such as your stove setup and specific meals. If you do any warm-up hikes in advance of the TCT or BBT, pay close attention to your fuel consumption to more accurately estimate your needs. You can conserve fuel when cooking by using a lid and windscreen, rehydrating your food in cold water for a half hour before cooking, and closely monitoring your meals to make sure the stove is not on any longer than it needs to be.

Water Treatment

Water treatment is almost a non-factor on these trails. Natural water sources are not reliable enough to depend on them being available when you need them. You will be using piped water sources where the water is already treated, so any water treatment gear will be dead weight in your pack. I did carry water treatment drops, hoping to use them on a natural source but never had the opportunity. It may feel strange leaving home without any water treatment gear, so if you need some peace of mind, carry something minimal like water treatment drops.

Water Storage

Water storage is very important on these trails, because you will be carrying and drinking a lot of water. Plan on at least a capacity of five to six liters. You will rarely carry that much water, but if you have to carry six liters only once, you need to have the capacity.

There are two primary means of achieving water capacity, hydration bladders and water bottles. Hydration bladders carry large volumes of water and have a hose to allow you to drink while hiking. Water bottles carry less water in each container and need to be removed from your pack to use.

My Choice: I use a combination of the two. I prefer water bottles, because I can easily see how much water I have left in my pack and can consume a lot of water at once to hydrate quickly. It is very important to know how much water you have consumed and how much remains in your pack on these trails. When you are 5 miles into an 11-mile stretch between water sources, you should know exactly how much water you have left to cover the remaining miles. A quick check of your water bottle will give you that info. A hydration bladder requires taking off your pack, taking out the bladder, checking the level, forcing the bladder back in a fully packed backpack, and then putting your pack back on.

I like hydration bladders as a secondary option. I carry one that has three liters of capacity but only use it on the longest stretches between water sources. My main beef with hydration bladders is that they stay packed away and you don't realize how little water you still have until you are completely out. It is also very easy to set your pack down on top of the hose and have all your water leak out onto your pack.

Water bottles are very convenient to drink from, fill up at sources, and put back in your pack to keep you moving. Reusing old plastic soda or sports drink bottles will weigh less than a sturdy name-brand water bottle. Sports drink bottles weight just over one ounce while a hard plastic or metal bottle weighs six ounces or more. If you carry two or three, you could be adding a pound to your pack just in empty bottles.

Another important note is that water is the heaviest item you will carry. It weighs 2.2 pounds per liter, so 5 liters of water would add 11 pounds to your back. Water does you no good on your back though, you need to be drinking it. Use the weight savings as motivation to hydrate. What you don't want is to repeatedly show up to water sources with an extra liter or two of water – you just carried an extra couple of pounds for no reason.

Take note of how much water you have left at each water source and do a rough calculation of the miles you just walked versus the volume of water consumed. Use this rough estimate to predict your water needs throughout the trip while adjusting for things like elevation change, temperature, and cooking needs that may increase your water demands.

[**i**] Start out carrying one liter for every three miles to the next source and adjust from there. Drink at least a liter at every water source as well. That's free water you don't have to carry!

e. First Aid

Your first aid kit will only be as useful as your own first aid knowledge. Ask yourself what type of injuries or ailments you are expecting and capable of treating. You may be able to clean a cut, but a more serious injury will require specialized equipment and care that you may not be capable of providing. Try and cover a lot of basics with very few items and understand that, if anything goes seriously wrong, you will be moving as quickly as possible to the nearest road and proper medical attention. You will probably not repair your own sprained ankle enough to continue your hike using anything in your first aid kit. You can, however, treat a blister and make your miles for the day in slightly less pain. Think of the first aid kit like any other piece of gear, you are facilitating hiking and preventing or addressing obstacles that get in the way of hiking, like blisters. Knowing how to read a map and find the closest road may help you more in an emergency than anything in your first aid kit.

First Aid – General

- Moleskin or other blister treatment – Most moleskin requires being cut to size. Consider how you will cut the fabric while on the trail and, if necessary, bring a small pair of scissors. Bring medical tape to help secure the moleskin to your foot, because the moleskin adhesive is not likely to last very long in a hiking shoe over miles of trail.

- Duct tape – Wrapped around trekking poles for storage. Has multiple uses.

- Knife – Don't get too carried away with your knife. You will probably rarely, if ever, use it. Ask yourself what scenario would require a knife and bring an appropriately-sized knife.

- Anti-bacterial ointment – For preventing infection on open cuts and scrapes.

- Personal medication – If you take medication on a regular basis, know that physical activity may result in a situation where you require medication. If you have serious allergic reactions, bring the appropriate medications with you.

First Aid – Optional

The following items could be useful in certain situations but are not essential. Only bring what you know how to use.

- Band-aids and/or gauze

- Pain relieving gels/creams (with Camphor, Menthol, Arnica)

- Anti-inflammatories and/or pain relievers (e.g., ibuprofen)

- Antihistamines

- Vitamins or dietary supplements

f. Personal Care

Below are items recommended for maintaining hygiene and protection from the elements while on the trail. Look in convenience store travel sections for smaller, travel-sized portions of these products. Creams and liquids carried add a lot of weight, especially for something you will use infrequently, so carry only what you think you will need by transferring bulk quantities into smaller containers.

- Sunscreen (SPF 30 and up)

- Lip balm (with SPF)

- Toothbrush & toothpaste

- Toilet paper & hand sanitizer

Optional:

- Insect repellent – You probably will not need this on these trails. The dry climate is not good for bugs.

- Wet wipes – Great for cleaning your feet at the end of a long day and maintaining hygiene in general.

- Ear plugs – Depends on your sensitivity to ambient noises.

g. Other Essentials

The following items can greatly enhance your hiking experience and some should be considered essential, such as a compass and headlamp. This list is not comprehensive to include all possible items that could be used in the backcountry. There are infinite options for creature comforts or personal affections to carry, which may be fun, but the items included here are the most likely to be carried and should strongly be considered for your own gear list.

Camera

Documenting your trip, and any strange and beautiful encounters along the way, preserves forever your memories and experiences for your own personal reminiscing or to share with others. There are many camera makes and models available to fulfill this role. Discussing all the possible options along with their individual advantages and drawbacks goes beyond the scope of this book. If you are interested in learning more about choosing appropriate camera equipment for your trip and advancing your hiking photography skills in general, I recommend checking out the following book:

Plan & Go | Hiking Photography: All you need to know to take better pictures on every trail (Sandiburg Press, 2017)

One downside of carrying a camera is that it not only adds weight but may lead to more accessories finding their way into your pack as your hobby expands. These could include extra lenses, a tripod, extra batteries and memory cards, lens filters, various lens and sensor cleaners, and charging cords. At the very least, a case should be carried to protect your equipment. Try to have a storage arrangement that prioritizes convenience and accessibility. Store your camera somewhere that will allow you to quickly grab a photo if an opportunity arises, without having to pull the camera from your pack. Your backpack's hip pockets may not be the best place to store your camera, because you can easily forget it's there as you throw your pack down to take a rest.

Compass

Essential, infallible, and affordable navigation device. Get used to using it while you know your location, so you are prepared for when you are lost. Practice comparing the topography on a map to the landscape around you. Try to find your location on a map. These are essential skills that will save you the weight of a GPS device and trouble when your GPS fails.

Headlamp

Bring one that uses the same batteries as any other battery-powered gear, so you can interchange them and share spare batteries. Headlamps do not need to be incredibly bright. Most available models will do the trick, so focus on weight, price, and battery compatibility if buying a new headlamp.

Map/Guidebook

Consult the map suggestions in Chapters 2 and 3 for specific recommendations on maps for the TCT and BBT, respectively. Of course, bring important pages of this guidebook with you. To go ultralight, copy the pages you will need to reference on the trail, like elevation profiles, data tables, contact info, etc. A zip lock bag is a great waterproof way to store your maps, although if the weather is nice, it is easier to access your maps from a hip belt pocket or shorts pocket and keep the zip lock stored away in case of rain.

Money/ID

Rarely will you need this but good to have anyways in case you are presented with the option of buying some extra food and snacks somewhere. A small resealable plastic bag works great as a lightweight wallet.

Sunglasses

These are potentially very sunny hikes. Bring a pair of sunglasses. Polarized lenses reduce glare from the sun, especially off reflective surfaces like the ocean, which is inescapable on these hikes.

Bandana

Easily the most versatile item in your pack with very little weight sacrificed. Clean up messes, handle hot cookware, shade yourself from the sun, get sweat out of your face, and potentially use it for first aid purposes.

Portable Charger (optional)

Carrying electronics, such as a phone, camera, portable media player, and GPS, are great to enhance the trail experience. But if you are relying on them a lot, you could run out of battery power quickly. A portable charger stores a charge in a small device that can then recharge depleted electronics, usually through a USB connection. Their capacity is measured in milliampere hours (mAh). Higher mAh means more charge for your device. 5,000 mAh is a good starting point and should give you three full charges on a smartphone. Some smartphones have cases available that have built-in battery storage. If you only need battery power for your phone, a specialized case would be a great option.

[**i**] Keep your phone in airplane mode while hiking to conserve battery and keep it available for photos or quick reference.

Gear Repair Kit (optional)

Depending on the condition of your gear, you may not need this item. Personally, I run my gear into the ground and extend it beyond its life expectancy by making small repairs as they occur to avoid a full replacement. A long section of duct tape serves as your first option for gear repair, and occasionally first aid, and can be stored by wrapping it around your trekking pole or other piece of gear. A small sewing kit of a needle and thread can repair rips in your pack, sleeping bag, clothing, or shoes without much weight cost. Develop a new skill and save yourself a lot of money by repairing rather than replacing gear.

Umbrella (optional)

Hiking umbrellas are another solution to the dilemma of protecting yourself from the sun while also ventilating your body. Hiking umbrellas are lightweight, plastic, and usually have a reflective canopy. They allow air to circulate your upper body while hiking and provide shelter during rest stops along the trail. Any umbrella will work, although hiking-specific ones will probably be the lightest and most durable.

7. Personal Experience

The previous chapters covered logistics and planning for your hike. This chapter documents my personal experience with planning and hiking the TCT and BBT for a look at how an actual hike of these trails plays out. In the first section, Plan, I present my personal planning strategy and the decisions that went into my hiking schedule as well as the food and gear I carried. The following section, Go, is a day-by-day account of my TCT and BBT hikes.

a. Plan

Logistics – Trans-Catalina Trail

From my last experience hiking the TCT, I knew that ferry schedules and campgrounds would be the major factors for my hiking plan. Additionally, I would have a hiking partner and had to consider everyone's schedule and ambitions for the hike. Following the steps outlined in Chapter 5 *Planning & Preparation*, I quickly determined my big-picture hiking plan.

1) Coordinate with potential hiking partners

There was some interest from a few friends but ultimately it would just be me and my girlfriend on this hike. She deferred to me for setting the pace of the hike as long as it wasn't too crazy. Based on many hikes with her in the past, I had a good feel for our comfort range on a hike like the TCT.

2) Estimate days on the trail

This was mostly constrained by work schedules so easy to determine. With four days available and based on my past experience, I was confident we would have no problem completing the trail in that time.

3) Determine availability and desired time of year

Based on our work schedules, we both only had certain days available, so those were the days we would be hiking. Fortunately, it was out of the heat of the summer, but unfortunately not during wildflower season.

4) Check camping availability

I checked the campsite availability online and saw that Parsons' Landing was half booked up, so I reserved that site first. It only has eight sites. The rest of the campgrounds had more availability, so I was not as worried about them filling up, especially outside of the busy time of year.

5) Book travel

I was able to reserve tickets online for the ferries, but had a dilemma about returning to my car. My preferred departure was out of Long Beach, and the only return from Two Harbors went to the San Pedro port. My plan was to take a ride service between San Pedro and Long Beach upon my return to the mainland. I booked one ticket out of Long Beach and a return to San Pedro, but right before I left for the trip, I got an extra day off work. With the extra day, I could head to the island a day early from San Pedro at any time and spend time in Avalon before hiking early the next day for Blackjack. The ferry company allowed me to transfer my ticket to a different day and port at no charge

My Itinerary

My itinerary was easy to determine based on my last hike. I knew I would have to stay at Blackjack Campground coming out of Avalon. I thought I would have to start hiking first thing off the ferry so would not have enough time to go further than Blackjack. I also remembered how beautiful Little Harbor was and how much I regretted not staying there for a night. I made sure to book a night there. From Little Harbor, it is only 5.2 miles to Two Harbors, which was too short of a distance, so the only other campground to book was Parsons' Landing. I wasn't yet sure if I was going to do Starlight Beach the day I got to Parsons' or the next day, when I had to catch my return ferry, but could make that decision the day of. At the last minute, I got an extra day to spend on the island on the front end of my trip and booked a night at Hermit Gulch Campground.

In the end, my campsites were Hermit Gulch (a last-minute addition), Blackjack, Little Harbor, and Parsons' Landing.

Logistics – Backbone Trail

Without ferries to worry about on the BBT, my main constraint was camping availability. Following the steps outlined in Chapter 5 *Planning & Preparation*, I quickly determined my big-picture hiking plan.

1) Coordinate with potential hiking partners.

I was going to hike the BBT by myself so did not need to do any coordination with others, just decide what kind of pace and direction I was looking for.

2) Estimate days on the trail

This was mostly constrained by work schedules so easy to determine. I had four days available and was confident I could hike the BBT in that time, since my last hike was in a shorter amount of time.

3) Determine availability and desired time of year

Work schedules made this a simple decision as well. I only had a few days available for both the TCT and BBT hike. I decided, for no particular reason, to do the TCT first, so the remaining days I had available off from work were the days I would be hiking the BBT. Ideally, I would have hiked during wildflower season.

4) Check camping availability

Circle X Ranch and Danielson Ranch were not available when I wanted to hike, so I had to look elsewhere for a place to stay on the west side of the trail. I looked up vacation rentals and found Cleft of the Rock Ranch, who allowed me to camp for the night. It was fortunate because my schedule was so tight that I did not have many options. I could have switched direction and hiked eastbound, bringing me to Circle X Ranch on a different day when it was potentially available. There were many sites available at Malibu Creek State Park and Musch Trail Camp is walk-in without a reservation system.

5) Book travel

I did not have to book much travel in advance, since I would be travelling from my home in Los Angeles. The day of the hike, I shuttled my truck to the Ray Miller Trailhead and then got dropped off at the Will Rogers Trailhead to hike back to my vehicle. I did not place any caches, which I did use for my last BBT hike.

My Itinerary

The last time I hiked the BBT, I went eastbound. For no other reason than to experience it the other way, I wanted to go westbound. Due to the limited camping on the BBT, I had easy decisions to make for the campgrounds I would take. I would be starting the day after finishing the TCT and was not planning an early start. The 10 miles to Musch Trail Camp would be perfect. From there, the next campground was Malibu Creek State Park, a reasonable day's hike for me. It got tricky from there though because Circle X Ranch is over 30 miles and a group campground. I called and asked very nicely if I could camp at Circle X Ranch and, although permission was granted, I did not actually go online to book the campsite for another day. By then, someone else had already reserved it. It's possible that it was a group who would have allowed me to stay, but I decided to look around at my other options. I found Cleft of the Rock Ranch, which would be a much more reasonable day from Malibu Creek State Park, and from there, I could reach the Ray Miller Trailhead the next day.

My campsites were Musch Trail, Malibu Creek State Park, and Cleft of the Rock Ranch. I only had to make an online reservation at Malibu Creek. I could have taken one of the walk-in sites at Malibu Creek, because, although there were people at the campground, it was nowhere near full. If my schedule had allowed, I would have stayed a night at La Jolla Valley Walk-in Camp.

Food – General

Food can add 10 pounds or more to your pack, so my meal planning focuses on avoiding carrying extra food. To know exactly the number of meals I need to carry, I create a grid with the number of days I will be hiking as columns and the meals as rows. Then I go through each day and mark the meals required for each day. For my first day on the trail, I don't need to bring a breakfast. For my last day on the trail, I don't need to bring a dinner. If you start your hike late in the day or finish early, you don't need to carry a lunch. My plan for the Backbone Trail is shown below as an example.

Meal	Nov. 11	Nov. 12	Nov. 13	Nov. 14	Total
Breakfast		x	x	x	3
Lunch	x	x	x	x	4
Snack	x	x	x	x	4
Dinner	x	x	x		3

Table 12 – Personal Backbone Trail Meal Plan

From the table above, I need 3 breakfasts, 4 lunches, 4 snacks, and 3 dinners to cover four days and three nights on the trail. An example of the food I carried for each meal is shown below.

Meal	Food	Quantity
Breakfast	Pastries	1-2 per day depending on size
	Coffee	A couple of scoops per day
Snacks	Granola bars	3 per day
	Fruit snacks	2 per day
	Candy bars	1 per day
	Chips or crackers	0.5-1 bag per day depending on size
Lunch	Tuna pouches	1 per day
	Tortillas	2 per day
	Peanut butter and jelly	1-2 oz each per day
Dinner	Dehydrated meals	1 pouch of 4oz-6oz per day

Table 13 – Personal Food Choices and Quantities

Personally, I barely touched the granola bars. Maybe I have reached a breaking point with them because I usually use them all the time as an on-the-go snack that gives me energy without having to stop and take off my pack. I never once wanted one on either trail. Also, chocolate does not hold up on these trails. But melted or not, it tastes the same, so I was still happy to have it. Otherwise, I was satisfied with my food selections, just would have brought slightly less granola bars.

Training – General

I did not do any training specifically for these trips. I hike a lot in my free time and can gauge my fitness based on how well I handle a day hike. I felt confident I was ready for these two multi-day trips based on my performance on shorter day hikes and knowledge gained from my previous hikes of both trails.

Gear – General

My philosophy towards gear is minimalist first and luxury second, meaning I go as light as possible on all the essentials, so I can carry a few unessential items without overburdening myself. The mild and stable climate of these two trails allowed me a much greater margin of error for my lightweight clothing and sleeping gear. I knew there was essentially no chance of freezing or even cold temps and virtually no chance of precipitation. An ultralight hiker's dream.

I was able to start both trails with gear I already possessed. There are no specialized gear items required for these trails. If you have the basics, you should be covered. But this is also a great opportunity to try ultralight gear and get comfortable carrying less.

The gear I carried is described in the table below. I am very comfortable sleeping out in the elements, I prefer it even, and carry less than most people might be comfortable with. This is the gear that works for me and, although most of my gear list might not fit with your hiking style, hopefully there is something new you can take away from it.

Gear Item	Comments
Backpack	Frameless ultralight pack with over 3,000 miles on it. My pack has seen better days but still gets the job done and only weighs one pound. It is an older design with only one main body pocket and three mesh side pockets for storage so not great for organization, but it can fit a lot of gear if you need it while other ultralight packs have limited volume. The pack uses a Thermarest Z-rest pad as the frame and is only compatible with a few types of mattresses for use as a frame. Because it is frameless, it requires more careful packing. Gossamer Gear G4 w/ hip belt pocket. 16.5 oz., 54 liters, $90.
Trekking poles	Off-brand trekking poles I bought online and have put about 2,000 miles on after my last pair of off-brand trekking poles broke. I prefer the latch lock system rather than the twist lock system. It is a little more expensive, but the twist lock always seems to break or frustrate very easily. You can find very cheap options online for half the price of name brand. However, buy at your own risk. These double as my shelter support poles, so they must be adjustable, otherwise I might still be using old ski poles. Cascade Mountain Tech Quick Lock Trekking Poles. 16 oz. (pair), $45.
Shelter	TCT: Two-person freestanding backpacking tent with separate bug net and rainfly. This is a little heavier than I like to go, but it provides peace of mind for those not yet comfortable with sleeping completely open to the elements, like my hiking partner. Picked this one up cheap from a garage sale! Big Agnes Copper Spur UL2: 3 lbs. 2 oz., 29 sq. ft., $150.

BBT: Solo tarp with groundsheet. Catenary cut ridgeline for the tarp. It can be confining when set up in "storm mode", i.e., staked tight to the ground, but, unless I am anticipating inclement weather, I can set it up higher off the ground or raise up one side for easy entry. A tarp has a million different setup options using a combination of trees, tent stakes, and trekking poles. I have used this tarp in the past for shade in sunny, exposed conditions or shelter from hail and rain but did not have to use it at all on this trip. I also carry 8 tent stakes (MSR Groundhogs). Tarp: Oware CatTarp 1.5, 10 oz., 9' long, 7'1" wide in front, 5'4" wide in rear when flat, $115. Stakes: 4 oz., $25. Groundsheet: 4 oz., free. |

Sleeping bag	Homemade down backpacking quilt. Not sure exactly what the warmth rating and weight on this is, since I made it myself, and it is far from a perfect build. I love it though. Has over 3,000 miles on it despite my poor sewing skills. Seems light, I estimate about 20 ounces based on the amount of down I put in it. Have taken it below freezing with a silk sleeping bag liner to help with drafts. Without the sleeping bag liner, it is great for the summer or mild weather like Southern California. 20 oz. (estimate), 35 degrees rating (estimate), materials cost about $200.
Sleeping pad	Closed-cell foam pad that fits into my pack as the frame support. Light, no risk of puncture, so I can throw it down anywhere during breaks, and it's comfortable enough. 10 oz., R-value of 2.6, $35.
Stove & fuel*	One of my luxury items. Isobutane canister stove with pot. Could have gone with an alcohol stove for less weight, but this one is so easy and heats up fast. After using it to cook for two on the TCT, I kept it for the BBT. Stove: 5.9 oz., $80. Fuel: 7 oz. (3.53 oz. of fuel), $5.
Cookware & utensils	Insulated pot that came with the stove system, 1-liter volume. I carried a coffee press that fits with the stove system and was maybe my favorite item I carried. Plastic spoon. Pot: 9.3 oz., included with stove. Coffee press: 0.8 oz., $15.
Water treatment	Not necessary, but I did carry water treatment drops. Never used them. 2 oz., $15.
Hydration system	One 3-liter hydration bladder with hose, two 1-liter water bottles (wide-mouth), three half-liter water bottles (light plastic). Hydration bladder: 7.2 oz., $35. Water bottles: 1.2 oz. to 0.6 oz., free.
Camera*	My big luxury item(s). Mirrorless camera with two lenses. Lenses are stored in padded case inside a waterproof bag. I also carried extra batteries, tripod, and memory cards. I don't want to count how many ounces and dollars this is!
Charger*	Portable battery pack with cords for camera and phone. One charge lasted for each trip, and I recharged my phone battery twice each time.
Phone*	Smartphones are extremely versatile items with multiple uses. Phone, camera, GPS, flashlight, media player, alarm clock, journal, unlimited knowledge database, etc. 5 oz. with case.
Map/map app	TCT: Printed the official map from the Catalina Conservancy as well as my own maps and elevation profile from CalTopo. BBT: Trails Illustrated Santa Monica Mountains map as well as my own maps and elevation profile from CalTopo.
Light source	Headlamp that uses a single AA battery. Carried one extra battery for the TCT, then replaced my battery and carried no extras for the BBT. 2.9 oz. with battery, $64.

* Luxury Items

Table 14 – Personal Gear Items and Comments

b. Go

Trans-Catalina Trail

The following is a day-by-day account of my thru-hike of the TCT.

Day 1 – October 7, 2016: Avalon to Hermit Gulch CG (11.7 miles)

The day had arrived and, of course, I still wasn't ready. The night before was spent sorting food and sewing rips in my pack, and I was still scrambling to get maps printed this morning. I was supposed to be the prepared hiker, taking my girlfriend, Yvonne, on her first thru-hike. She has been out for overnights and up 10,000-foot peaks but not for more than two days and nowhere near the roughly 50 miles we planned.

Thankfully, there was no traffic once we hit the road to San Pedro. I got an extra day off work at the last minute and could reschedule our ferry for a day earlier that now returned to the same port. Plenty of parking and time at the port to pick up my hardcopy ticket at the desk. The ferry left on time and cruised past a large battleship and the shipyards of Long Beach. As soon as we were in open water, a pod of dolphins swam by the ferry. Just a little further along, cormorants and other sea birds were feeding on a massive school of fish.

Gradually, the island came into view. First as a pale-blue mountainous silhouette and then the coastline's steep cliffs showed themselves. It was a perfect day. When we hit the dock, we still did not have a plan for the day. I had a reservation at Hermit Gulch Campground, which I also had made last-minute when my schedule opened up, but that was only 1.7 miles from us and it was 11:00 AM. We decided that lunch was first, then hiking plans.

Figure 33 – Leaving San Pedro | Walking into Avalon

A quick call to the Two Harbors Visitor Center confirmed my camping reservations. Then we took a seat at a restaurant on the beach. Baseball playoffs were just starting. It was tempting to watch them at the bar all day before stumbling to Hermit Gulch Campground, but the next day's hike to Blackjack Campground was looming over us. I knew from my last hike of the TCT that it can be a brutal climb.

Your pack is at its heaviest to start out, full of food and the water to get you 10.5 miles to Haypress Reservoir, and there is little shade. If we could drop our gear off at Hermit Gulch, then slackpack (hike with day packs) the east end of the island back to Hermit Gulch, it would break the hike into two days and make the climb so much easier. We decided to save our money and head for Hermit Gulch with the hope that one of the many golf carts cruising by might pick us up on the way, since we were definitely going to be pushing daylight at the end of the day.

No such luck on the way up. We passed some mule deer and acorn woodpeckers at the golf course on our way to the campground, with one buck walking right alongside of us for 100 feet. Once we arrived, we quickly set up our tent and repacked our bags with just water and food to get us back to Hermit Gulch, then headed back down to Avalon and the trailhead. This time, we did get lucky with a golf cart ride, Yvonne's first hitch-hike, for about a half mile from some friendly folks from Los Angeles.

Figure 34 – Golf Carts in Avalon | View of Avalon and Harbor

The walk up Wrigley Road from Avalon took us past a pet cemetery, the Mt. Ada residence, and an awesome view of Avalon and the harbor. We spotted a yellow submarine, seriously, trolling the shoreline way below us. There were lots of folks driving carts through this area for views, but once we stepped on the TCT at the Renton Mine Trailhead, we didn't see another person for the rest of our hike that day and into the night.

It was 4:00 PM when we left the trailhead, and we had 7.5 miles back to Hermit Gulch Campground. I immediately felt amazing about our decision to do this climb today, because the position of the sun to the west of the island at this hour was enough to shade almost the entire trail in the shadow of the ridge above us.

We saw more mule deer, including a large buck standing guard over a fire break near the top of the climb. We took a long rest at East Mountain and took in the views of the mainland, the San Gabriel Mountains, Santa Monica Mountains, and San Clemente Island to the south. A fox barked in the distance, somewhere in the sea of prickly pear cacti all around us.

Figure 35 – Yvonne & Sam at Eastern Terminus | Sunset over Western Coastline

The sun was getting lower as we cruised the pleasant open spaces above Avalon. At one turn, we both stopped in our tracks as our first view of the island's western coastline came into view with the setting sun casting purple, orange, and pink around it. Stunned by our surroundings, we watched the sun push over the horizon and little dots of light began to speckle the mainland.

There was still light at dusk, but it was fading quickly. We took the trail down through Wrigley Memorial and Botanical Garden, since it was completely dark at that point and would save us a little time. The memorial was framed by a halo in the moonlight, making a stoic building suddenly spooky. In the dark, I reminded myself that there were no predators on the island to harm me. The gate at the garden entrance was closed, so we were kind of locked in, but fortunately found a way to slip through. I would pay my fare tomorrow. It was too dark to see any of the plants anyway. We reached camp, got into camp shoes, ate the leftovers from lunch, and cooked a dinner.

We have some backtracking to get up to the TCT again so have added miles to our trip overall but shaved a third off tomorrow's miles and can carry less water coming out of camp. The east end of the hike ended up being smooth and nice after I was dreading the climb somewhat. Hiking with a daypack and in the shade made the difference.

Day 2 – October 8, 2016: Hermit Gulch CG to Blackjack CG (10.4 miles)

Yesterday's slackpack really paid off today. We could sleep in. I'm pretty sure, I did not move once in my sleep. I think I had some to catch up on. The late start meant the sun was blazing already as we made our coffee and packed up. I checked out the Nature House right across from the campground. They had some good exhibits on the natural history of the island as well as a variety of maps. We then started to head back up to the TCT through the Wrigley Memorial and Botanical Gardens and paid the $7 entrance fee this time.

The garden was somewhat subdued, but that's to be expected in early October. The plants are still waiting on the first big rain after a long, dry summer to wake up for the winter growing season. There were amazing cacti from all over the world and a close look at some of the native Catalina Island species. We were feeling the sun by the time we reached the TCT. There were a few other people hiking this section, which is part of a popular loop out of Avalon. After we left the shade structure at Hermit Gulch Summit, we were alone again.

Figure 36 – Wrigley Botanic Garden

Soon, our first views of Mt. Orizaba and Black Jack Mountain, which would be our destination for the day, our last view of Avalon, and an awesome view of the San Pedro Channel full of boats were all before us. We also saw our first signs of bison. Footprints and scat appeared around the trail. The route broke from the dirt road and past an animal management fence before reaching Haypress Reservoir, where a bison was lounging in the back of the bone-dry reservoir. All the picnic tables at Haypress Reservoir were in the sun, so we took lunch in the shade of a large pine. We would hear tidbits of information amplified from passing eco tours. They were searching for bison. Maybe I should use a loudspeaker to find more bison.

Figure 37 – Orizaba and Blackjack ahead | San Pedro Channel View

An acorn woodpecker perched on the water fountain and drank from leaks in the standpipe. As soon as we left lunch, we saw three bison right off the trail. One was taking a dirt bath. On our way to Blackjack, the climbs in sun-exposed terrain got to us. These are not well-engineered trails that utilize switchbacks for climbing and descending the terrain. We took a break in the only shade around, a small bush next to the trail. Not long after, there was a huge oak tree shading a bench that would have made a much better stopping point, where we ran into two day hikers. They were the only people we have run into on the trail outside of the campgrounds and Hermit Gulch/Wrigley Memorial area.

Another switchback-less climb and we were at Blackjack Campground. Walking up to camp, about 20 Catalina California quail appeared and hustled across the trail into an oak tree. There were a few groups of campers already at the campground, and I realized I wasn't sure what site number I had reserved. Turns out there was cell service, and I had selected a site far from where most of the people were set up. A huge oak covered the site and invited us in. A little deer passed through, then bounded away. After dinner, two Catalina foxes scurried past the edge of our site and one stopped to stare at Yvonne, before disappearing into the dark.

Figure 38 – Hiking the Interior | Blackjack Campground

Even though we split up the mileage between today and yesterday, it was a strenuous day baking in the sun. Yvonne performed amazingly, climbing and descending in the heat all day. Tomorrow should be nice and easy.

Day 3 – October 9, 2016: Blackjack CG to Little Harbor (7.2 miles)

We had a very pleasant day and hike into Little Harbor, despite the sun's efforts to make it difficult. Again, we slept in enough that the sun was in full force when we started. Yvonne saw a bison walking through the campground in the morning. With no rush to make 7.2 miles to camp, we spent some time stretching in the shade before starting out, something I don't do enough of.

Once we left Blackjack Campground and hit the saddle between Mt. Orizaba and Blackjack Mountain, we could see much of the island ahead of us. It did not take long to hike to the airport, passing some native Tongva people's sites on the way. There is a huge cactus garden at the entrance to the airport. It was a little early in the day for lunch, but we had to order something from the grill at the airport. Tri-tip sandwich and some fries with a soda. For water to carry out, we were told they don't have a spigot available due to the drought, but we could fill up in the restroom sink.

There was a huge map made of tile outside the entrance to the airport on a shelf, about two feet high, maybe 20-25 feet across that illustrated the whole island. We were ready to get to the beach and relax for the afternoon. Just past the airport, a couple more bison crossed the trail in front of us. They were not as interested in us as we were in them.

We took a little break before the long descent to the ocean and Little Harbor. For whatever reason, I tied my bandana around my neck rather than have it under my hat when leaving the break. We walked for a good while conversing about silly far-off subjects down the steep trail, when I realized the bandana was no longer around my neck. I had over 7,000 miles of thru-hiking with that bandana. It was a rag full of holes from singeing it in campfires and when I cut out eyeholes to prevent snow blindness after losing my sunglasses in Colorado's snowy San Juan Mountains. I placed it in my pack at age 20, preparing for the Appalachian Trail, and it has not left in the nine years since. No matter how steep the hill was I just climbed down, I was going back up to recover my sweat-covered rag.

Figure 39 – Airport in the Sky | Tile Map of Catalina Island

Of course, it was all the way back where we took a break. I probably didn't make it 10 feet before it fell off. It was sitting in the middle of the trail at the top of the open gentle ridge that looked out to the San Pedro Channel, the west end of the Island including Silver Peak, and the Pacific Ocean. I ran back to Yvonne waving the bandana over my head in victory.

We were ready to get to the beach. We cruised down into Little Harbor before 3:00 PM and went to Shark Harbor first, just south of Little Harbor. There was a guy lounging with his dog at a picnic bench above the beach but otherwise this side of the harbor was ours. I got in the ocean immediately. The beach was clean and the water cold. Jumping in fresh off the hot trail felt therapeutic, like the feeling you get going from a hot tub to a cold pool.

As soon as we had dunked ourselves, we looked back to see our unguarded packs invaded by a seagull. After chasing him off a few times, he finally got the tortillas he was after. Yvonne wandered off to explore the rocks between Little Harbor and Shark Harbor, while I did my best to eat our packs lighter. We had a ton of granola bars that neither of us have touched, but I was doing work on the rest of our food. We can get resupply at Two Harbors if I get too carried away.

After our relaxation at Shark Harbor, we rinsed the sand off with a spigot on the beach and headed over to our campsite at Little Harbor via the trail over the Whale's Tail, a huge rock outcropping that splits the two harbors. There is a great view of the secluded beaches and rocky cliffs that make this place special. Our site was huge. We had a large shade structure with three picnic tables, water faucet, grill, fire pit with ring seating, trash can, and a massive palm tree to set our tent under. The wind was not bad at all. We could have been a little closer to the beach but this will do. I saw signs of bison again.

Figure 40 – Relaxing at Shark Harbor | Campground at Little Harbor

We set up the tent and then headed back to the Whale's Tail for sunset. At first, low clouds moved in and obscured the horizon, but eventually they cleared and the sky filled with vibrant orange, pink, purple, and blue colors that reflected onto the ocean below our perch. I am so glad we got to camp at Little Harbor. I passed through early in the morning on my last hike of the TCT and have been thinking about spending a day here ever since. The pace of the hike has been great. We have plenty of time during the day and have eased into this trail as much as you can. I think the hiker hunger is starting to kick in for Yvonne though. Luckily, she loves the trail dinners (who could be mad at cheddar broccoli rice and bacon bits).

We will need rest and sustenance for a big day tomorrow. Two big climbs before and after Two Harbors with more miles than any day so far, maybe the most Yvonne has done in a day before. We will need a balance of staying light on food and water plus fueling up a ton. An early start would help us out a lot.

Day 4 – October 10, 2016: Little Harbor to Parsons' Landing (18.0 miles)

We got out of camp just as the sun was rising over the east side of the island. From our campsite, we climbed up switchbacks, out of the shadows, to look down on Little Harbor. It was actually somewhat cold in the morning, but still not enough to require anything more than shorts. A solitary bison grazed on a hillside opposite us.

The climb was strenuous. With amazing coastline views and cooler morning temps, we did not stop until reaching a shade structure near the top. Little clouds were forming against the island's topography and then disappearing above the open ocean. The trail has been mostly dirt fire roads, which overwork parts of your leg due to repetitive motions. I was missing irregular single-track trail to evenly distribute the aches and pains over my whole leg. I was bothered by mild shin splints on the walk into Two Harbors while staring ahead at the climb up Silver Peak, knowing my long day was just beginning.

Figure 41 – West End View and Vast Ocean | Shade Structure above Little Harbor

In Two Harbors, we tried to quickly take care of any business to allow ourselves more time for the miles ahead. I picked up my locker key for Parsons' Landing and chatted with the Two Harbors Visitor Services staff about the trail on the west side of Silver Peak. I was trying to avoid the steep decline to Parsons' Landing on the TCT, but was worried I was walking into an even worse descent on the backside of Silver Peak judging from the map's topography. One of the staff members had hiked over Silver Peak and back as a day hike and agreed that, while it is steep, it wasn't much worse than the TCT route.

Confident that the route over Silver Peak was feasible, I left to find Yvonne at the grill reading over the lunch menu. We both put down a burger and then split a heavily-iced cinnamon bun on the porch in the company of a huge raven. It was tempting to take a little nap on the beach and digest lunch, but we still had almost 13 miles ahead of us and another tough climb that stood out in the memories of my last TCT hike. So we had heavy packs, loaded with all of our water for the rest of the day, and full stomachs heading out into the afternoon heat with shin splints still bothering me.

Once climbing, we stopped about every half mile, anywhere there was even a little bit of shade, until we ate away most of the steep part. Yvonne impressed me on this section. She's resting enough to not wear herself completely out, while keeping forward progress to push through the tough parts. I had to check my map. This climb was about 1,300 feet in less than 1.5 miles. It eased up a bit as we got closer to the trail up Silver Peak.

Figure 42 – Steep Climb up from Two Harbors | Silver Peak Summit View

We split from the official TCT route where it heads down to Parsons' Landing. From my last hike, I remember inching downhill on that section and wondering how it was possible to have a road that steep or any vehicles that could drive it. The trail to Silver Peak was nice but incredibly steep on the last hundred feet to the summit. We had an amazing 360-degree view of the island with no signs of human impact besides the fire road and old fence line below us. We had almost 7.5 miles and the steep decline of Silver Peak still ahead of us and were well into the afternoon, so the celebration up top was brief.

The trail west of Silver Peak remained elevated for some time. Wispy clouds draped the trail. One look over my shoulder caught an amazing cliff above the coastline that was pinning the clouds against it. We finally reached the decline I had been concerned about, and it ended up being just as I hoped, clear and no steeper than the TCT section. We had to take our time, but it was safe. Once we reached the TCT again at the bottom, we set down our packs and headed for Starlight Beach.

It hadn't struck us that the end of the trail was only one mile ahead. We had been so occupied with the ocean views and strenuous climbs that it stayed off our mind. Plus, as Yvonne pointed out, we still had a lot of miles left to truly be done, so it felt a little unfulfilling. On the way to Starlight, we thought we heard an eagle or osprey over the ridge. I had been told an eagle's nest was in the area, when I inquired about hiking West Peak, and not to disturb it.

I decided to take the opportunity to hike West Peak even though we were tight on time and at the end of a long day. I wanted to lay my eyes on the west end of the island, knowing I had walked there from the far east end. Being able to look back as far as you can see and know you got there under your own power is one of the pleasures of thru-hiking.

The off-trail detour to West Peak followed a faint use path through prickly pear covered slopes and razor ridgelines. I finally got the sight I was seeking, the rocky west point of the island slipping into the Pacific. To reach the farthest west point of the island at the ocean would have required some technical climbing and a lot more time. I left satisfied with the view from West Peak and the island behind me.

Figure 43 – Off Trail to West Peak | Looking East towards Rest of Island

We resumed our hike to Starlight Beach. The trail dropped steep downhill, making us rethink if we even wanted to finish the last few tenths of a mile if it meant having to climb back up. We had a celebration at the beach and took our photos, but I could tell it didn't feel like the end to Yvonne. We still had 4.6 miles back to Parsons' Landing, likely some in the dark.

The hike back to our packs at the Silver Peak Trail went fast. Immediately east of the Silver Peak Trail junction, the TCT takes a steep drop. I remember being frustrated by this on my last hike, because you gain the elevation right back again for no apparent reason. Coming from Parsons' Landing, there was a junction that immediately preceded the drop. I was hoping that trail connected through and avoided the pointless elevation change. Sure enough, there was a little worn road that, to me, seemed like that connection. Turns out that road had a huge washout or landslide that displaced the original road and created a huge jump at one point. Vehicles could no longer cross, so they routed the access road down and then back up around the washout, but we had no problem going straight through.

Figure 44 – Western Terminus | Yvonne and Sam at Starlight Beach

Now back on the TCT with an easy grade to Parsons' Landing, we could relax and take in the setting sun. Yvonne has done this hike in style. Today was a tough day, and she seemed to enjoy most of it, and the difficult sections never deterred her. She's gotten into the hiking routine. She's adept with the tent and stove and was even on the lookout for little seasoning packets from the grill in Two Harbors for our dinner today.

We walked under moonlight at the end of our stroll to Parsons'. It has been getting fuller every day. Yesterday half-moon, today waxing gibbous. Great for night hiking, bad for stars. When we reached the lockers at Parsons' above the beach and set our packs down to grab the water and firewood, Yvonne finally let out signs of relief and accomplishment. "We made it! We did it!" There was just the flat West End Road the next day, nothing compared to our day today, so it felt as though we were on our way.

We went for a quick rinse of our feet in the ocean. The beach was covered with tiny smooth pebbles at the water's edge that felt amazing on our feet. We rubbed them into our calves and ankles, and it felt like the best massage I've ever received. I wondered how much people across the San Pedro Channel in Los Angeles would pay for the ocean rock therapy we had free at our campsite.

Day 5 – October 11, 2016: Parsons' Landing to Two Harbors (7.5 miles)

We did it. Easy day that we made hard on ourselves. We only had the West End Road to Two Harbors but were aiming to make the early ferry, so we kept a brisk pace. Since I thought we had to make it by 11:00 AM, we had a quick morning at the site. We now have a rhythm together. Make coffee, put the food bag together, take photos, pack, put the tent away, more coffee, fill up water, pack some more, and then hike.

Nice clouds made the walk pleasant. A kestrel was perched on a wire not far off the trail, while a huge pod of dolphins fed off the coast behind it. We started picking up the pace at the end, hustling to get in before 11. But it turned out to be an 11:30 AM ferry, which gave us enough time to enjoy a beer on the beach at Two Harbors. Fortunately, there were no issues switching to the earlier ferry, otherwise we would have had to wait until 4:00 PM.

Figure 45 – Morning at Parsons' Landing | Victory Beers at the Beach

A few Bloody Marys on the ferry as we cruised back to San Pedro and the urban landscape surrounding Los Angeles. A pit stop at Jollibee for a bucket of chicken on the way home, then showers and preparing for the Backbone Trail the next day. I'm so glad Yvonne has been with me on this hike. She made a tough hike look easy, and we had a lot of fun sharing this amazing landscape. I'm gonna miss her on the Backbone Trail.

Backbone Trail

The following is a day-by-day account of my thru-hike of the BBT.

Day 1 – October 12, 2016: Will Rogers to Musch Trail CG (9.9 miles)

Time to start the next adventure. I gave myself four days to walk about 70 miles on the BBT, almost 20 miles more, but in one less day than I hiked the TCT with Yvonne. I would be hiking alone, but she helped shuttle my truck to the Ray Miller Trailhead in the morning.

When we reached the Will Rogers trailhead to start the hike, I realized that in switching from my two-person backpacking tent to my one-person tarp, I had forgotten a crucial element, my ground sheet. My tarp has no bottom, so that is the only interface with the ground besides my sleeping pad. It would take at least another hour or two to go retrieve it in traffic, and I just wanted to start hiking. I was reasonably confident that I would not see rain, so at least the ground would be dry if I were to sleep straight on the dirt.

I said goodbye and, not far beyond the trailhead, I climbed enough to gain an ocean view with the recently traversed Catalina Island behind me. The transition to wilderness was faster than expected, as I escaped the development and neighborhoods surrounding the park entrance.

With the TCT fresh on my mind, this first section of the BBT drew immediate comparisons. First, the climbing is so easy compared to the TCT. It's even pleasant! The single-track trail also makes you feel engulfed by the land-scape and vegetation. There is a lot more vegetation. The TCT seems barren by comparison. The plants around me were dry and dormant due to the season, but they still cast shade and filled my vision with colors and patterns.

Figure 46 – Start at Will Rogers Trailhead | Eagle Rock (from below)

As I gained elevation, I could look out to the wilderness. A nighthawk flew past and then later a northern flicker. Hikers were scarcer than the birds, although a few bikers rode past. As I approached Eagle Rock, day hikers called out and waved from one of the caves on the side of the rock.

It was such a nice walk to the camp, which was more spacious and pleasant than I expected. Why can't they have more of these?! It was empty when I arrived and one person rolled up after me. It was a colder night but still not uncomfortable. I laid down my sleeping pad on a patch of grass and crawled under my quilt to sleep with coyotes yipping in the distance.

Day 2 – Oct. 13, 2016: Musch Trail CG to Malibu Creek CG (15.6 miles)

I woke up to little towhees inspecting the campground, checking to see if everything was in order. They were firm but fair. I was covered in dew, a perk of cowboy camping. As I was walking out of camp, I met the other campers. They were also hiking the BBT! A couple, who were heading east, so only 10 miles from the end of their trip. The trail was just a few months old, so they were among the first to walk the official route. It sounded like the hike was going well, but they expressed that some of the water and camping logistics had made it difficult. They had hiked the distance between Circle X and Malibu Creek, which I will be breaking up. They had not seen anyone else out doing the whole trail.

I contacted my friend, Zach, who would meet me later in the day for a section of the trail. Cell service and frequent road crossings facilitate last-minute meetups. There were some deer over in Trippet Ranch, as a few people started their hikes for the day. The walk to Dead Horse Trailhead was pleasant. I picked up water and let Zach know my estimated time of arrival again. We agreed to meet on the trail somewhere between Dead Horse Trailhead at Topanga Highway and the next road not even a mile further at Old Topanga Canyon Road.

We both managed to get lost and missed each other in that short section. Once I did the steep climb up from Topanga Highway, lots of other trails started appearing and, at a motorway junction, there was no clear direction for the BBT. I cut down to some water tanks, where it looked like the trail should go, and realized, I probably walked past Zach at this point. The water tanks made a good landmark for a meetup, so I called him and we figured it out. I think the nearby elementary school uses the trails, and the BBT gets mixed in with their trails.

Across from Old Topanga Canyon Road, the trail was a very straightforward, single track that rose through oak woodlands and a few meadows full of golden grasses. The climbing was long and steady, and we kept a brisk pace thanks to all the shade. Great views of the cliffs around Topanga Lookout above us.

Figure 47 – Hiking Up to Stunt Road | Tapia Park

At Stunt Road, Zach headed back to the parking area at Old Topanga Canyon Road with about 4 miles to get back. I pushed up to Saddle Peak and took the side trail up for a view. The long descent had awesome rock formations and manzanita around the trail. It went on uninterrupted forever. When I made it to Malibu Canyon Road, I cut down through Tapia Park and straight to the campground. I wanted to check out the Rock Pools and Gillette Ranch but didn't have time for both.

Catching my breath at the campground for a second, I witnessed a bunch of small birds and squirrels come under fire from two larger birds, either hawks or owls, and start a chorus of squeals in the middle of the campground. Not ten minutes later, a cat appeared for another run at the helpless squirrels and birds. I realized it was a bobcat stalking prey. One squirrel in particular was super freaked out and loud. I had enough time to grab my camera and watch the hunt. I've hiked thousands of miles and seen less than five wild cats in all that time. Once the bobcat walked off, I left for the Rock Pools and ran into him again exiting the campground. The bobcat seemed more annoyed by me interrupting his dinner than scared, as he tucked back into the woods momentarily.

The sun had eased up as I walked through Malibu Creek Park to the Rock Pools. The creek floodplains were wide open with huge cliffs and peaks looking down on the grassy valley. I stumbled upon some people shooting a western scene by the creek. They were dressed in old-timey clothes next to a canvas tent with camera equipment all around. A couple of people were top-roping some of the outcroppings near the Rock Pools. When I arrived at the pools, a few more people climbed down from an area way behind the pool with a climbing rope. I got in the spirit and scrambled up the side of the pools to gain a better vantage point.

Figure 48 – Malibu Creek State Park | Moon over Malibu Creek Campground

It seemed like there were a lot of little cracks and side trails to explore in this area, but I was content with my view of the pools so headed back and settled in for the night. I got one more visit from the bobcat, who poked his head through my campsite and then did a lap around the campground.

Day 3 – Oct. 14, 2016: Malibu Creek CG to Cleft of the Rock Ranch (19.8 miles)

Huge day today, but I finished in a comfortable time. I was aided by an early start and low clouds protecting me from the sun for the climb out of Malibu Creek Camp. I threw all my things in my pack and started hiking without breakfast or coffee in order to get set up near the last water source for the day in Tapia Park. I would take my breakfast and coffee there, alone, in a huge day-use area under oak trees. I filled up on water for the day (4.5 liters) and headed out to the BBT by cutting through Malibu Creek rather than on the highway crossing. I found a good trail west of the bridge. It may have been the old BBT route before it was washed out by flooding. The creek had an ammonia smell from the sewage treatment plant just upstream.

The fog that encompassed me on the climb threw a blanket over the landscape once I reached the peaks. Mountain tops popped up like islands from the cloud layer. I made a detour up McAuley Peak, which required a minor rock scramble near the top. The ridges ahead would be enshrouded in clouds for one second, then revealed the next. I stood on the peak and thought about its namesake, Milt McAuley, and all the work he did to make the BBT a reality and that the trail was in a new phase of its existence with an exciting future, nearly 40 years after it was first conceived.

Figure 49 – Cloudy Morning | McAuley Peak Summit Block

The rest of the ridgewalk was outstanding. The curves and fins of the protruding Sespe Formation made me feel as though I was in Utah, not Los Angeles. Dropping off the ridge into Solstice Canyon, I really started to make miles. The tread was great and not too strenuous. At the Kanan Dume Road crossing, I ran into an Uber driver stretching his legs after dropping off some folks at one of the wineries nearby. I went looking for Newton Falls, but it was bone dry. Later in oak-covered Trancas Canyon, I did see a pool of water in the creek but it looked stagnant.

I pushed hard to get to Mulholland Highway, where I would end my day. Cleft of the Rock Ranch is near where the trail crosses Mulholland, and I had arranged to camp on the property, right off the BBT. I had enough cell service during the day to let them know an accurate time of arrival.

Figure 50 – Sespe Formation | Upper Solstice Canyon

I hadn't seen a mirror in a few days and did my best job of putting myself together before walking up to the ranch. I was warmly greeted, including from a few dogs and parrots, and welcomed up through the property. I got a tour of the area, which included a secluded grotto. In wetter months, the grotto has a flowing waterfall. I watched a little bird drink from the seeps in the cliff. I said goodbye when it started getting dark, knowing that I would be starting before the sun was up the next day. I planned an early start to give me plenty of time for side trips in addition to all the miles I had to cover to get back to my truck at the western terminus.

Day 4 – Oct. 15, 2016: Cleft of the Rock Ranch to Ray Miller TH (27.5 mi)

I got my early start. I was hiking before 5:00 AM under a full moon and did not need a headlamp. I found a trail from the grotto that led directly to the BBT. The connector trail seemed like it went right along the cliff above the grotto, but it was too dark at that time for me to know for sure. Once on the BBT, I was walking the wide and well-graded Etz Meloy Motorway with views of the moonlit landscape. The moon itself had been obscured by trees and ridges so far, but finally around one turn, it was suddenly revealed. It startled me. Bright, green, and hovering in the air, it caught me off guard. It looked so close, like it was sitting just at the end of the mountain range. I stopped to watch the moonset from above the clouds and then, not even five minutes later down the trail, as the view opened up east, I saw the glow of early dawn. Moonset and sunrise, almost simultaneously, was a new experience for me that I won't soon forget.

As the sky filled with light, the cloud layer remained. It covered the roads and towns below and draped the peaks in a mystical mist. Sandstone Peak was just ahead, and I wanted to summit while the clouds were still low. Thankfully, they waited for me, and I had one of the best views I've seen on Sandstone Peak. All the surrounding mountain peaks were poking through the sea of clouds like islands. I was excited for the rest of the hike down Sandstone Peak. The Boney Mountain formation is one of my favorite in all the Santa Monica Mountains. Rather than one prominent ridge, the high elevations are maintained over a massive area with little peaks scattered throughout and interesting rock forms popping out of the chaparral. It sits right above the ocean, with views of the Channel Islands and farmlands of Ventura County to the west, and picks up moisture off the ocean so always seems to be lusher than other parts of the mountain range.

I checked out Inspiration Point and was treated to views of huge volcanic intrusions. At the Tri-Peaks turnoff, I had to make a decision. There were caves rumored to be in the area, but I had never seen them in the few times I've been up Tri-Peaks. And searching around for caves could take some time. I was doing the math of how long the detour would take and delay my arrival at the Ray Miller Trailhead. Then I remembered that this was exactly why I had started hiking before the sun was even up. I don't know when I'll be back in this area, and here I am a half mile away. I headed out for the caves still with no idea how to find them.

Figure 51 – Sandstone Peak | Boney Mountain Formation

Certain they were not at the Tri-Peaks summit, I took a use trail away from the summit that dead-ended and was heading far from the ridgeline. Not so certain anymore, I headed back to the established trail and up to the summit while closely watching the trail for any side trails leading to secret caves. It dropped down into an overgrown area on the south side of the summit, but there was clearly a footpath, so I continued. There was some exposure on the other side of the summit before I started to see what looked like possible caves. Huge rocks were piled on top of one another with little gaps to crawl through. I picked one and headed inside the mountain to find a network of crawlspaces, paths, open areas, slots, and what looked like deep, dark caves. I stuck to the slots and eventually daylighted on the backside of the mountain. Rather than backtracking through the maze, I decided to climb over the mountain back to the Tri-Peaks Trail. It wasn't clear, but eventually I found the way.

I felt so happy to find these caves. I'm amazed they are not more popular. There is nothing else I've seen like it in the area. I could have spent hours there, but the image of a state park employee locking my car into the Ray Miller Trailhead parking lot was motivation to keep moving. The west side of the Boney Mountain formation was a long downhill with the Pacific

Ocean at the end, but I kept turning around to look at the volcanic cliffs behind me. They were massive and amazing, with irregular formations in shades of red and brown, like daunting gates to the Boney Mountain formation and the Santa Monica Mountains.

Figure 52 – Tri-Peaks Cave | Gates to Boney Mountain Formation

At Danielson Ranch, I did my best to lighten my pack by eating all the food with heavy-looking packaging. With trash cans there, I could toss the peanut butter and jelly jars and other trash that was not actually weighing me down, but it made me feel better. The sycamores are impressive in this area, dwarfing the oaks. My feet were starting to ask for some mercy at this point, but the end was nearing, and I wanted to keep going. I actually got some crazy clouds coming in that looked like rain but never manifested. I took a little detour to check out the La Jolla Valley Walk-in Camp. It was empty and secluded, I wished my day was ending there and I could soak in the solitude for the night. The massive meadow went beyond what my eyes could see from the walk-in camp. I will have to come back and explore the rest of La Jolla Valley another time.

Figure 53 – La Jolla Valley in the Distance | Sycamore at Danielson Ranch

Finally, I could see the coastline clearly below me and the Ray Miller Trailhead. The sun lit up the cliffs above the beach. It was a peaceful end to this hike. I walked switchbacks down with the ocean now closer and closer and kept reminding my sore feet that we were almost done. I was definitely too early for any risk of getting locked in the parking area. There were plenty of people still heading up the BBT for the views of the coast, as I was coming down. I got a few strange looks while taking photos with the unremarkable trailhead sign. I couldn't explain the feeling if I tried.

Figure 54 – Walking towards the Ocean | Arrival at Ray Miller Trailhead

A thru-hike can be shared through stories, journals, and photos. But those cannot convey the moment when you have an entire mountain range at your back and the memories of every step along the way filling your head. I headed down the coast and back to Los Angeles, past people sliding down huge hills of sand above the beach with the sun setting behind me.

Figure 55 – On the Beach before Driving Back to L.A.

Appendices

A. Sample Itineraries

Trans-Catalina Trail

Camp	6 Days (WB)		5 Days (WB)		4 Days (WB)		3 Days (WB)		4 Days (EB)	
	Day	Miles	Day	Miles	Day	Miles	Day	Miles	Day	Miles
Avalon									4	15.7
Hermit Gulch	1	12.3[1]								
Blackjack	2	9.2	1	15.7	1	15.7	1	15.7	3	7.2
Little Harbor	3	7.2	2	7.2					2	12.7[2]
Two Harbors (0.4 mi E)					2	12.7				
Parsons' Landing	4	11.8	3	11.8			2	19.0	1	12.8[3]
Starlight Beach (official terminus; no camp)										
Parsons' Landing	5	9.2	4	9.2	3	16.2				
Two Harbors	6	7.5	5	7.5	4	7.5	3	16.7		

[1] Drop packs at Hermit Gulch CG and hike eastern portion with day packs. Return to Hermit Gulch CG via Hermit Gulch Trail.
[2] Via West End Road | [3] Via Silver Peak and Starlight Beach

Backbone Trail

Camp	6 Days (WB)		5 Days (WB)		4 Days (WB)		3 Days (WB)		4 Days (EB)	
	Day	Miles	Day	Miles	Day	Miles	Day	Miles	Day	Miles
Eastern Terminus									4	25.5
Musch Trail	1	9.9	1	9.9	1	9.9				
Malibu Creek	2	15.6	2	15.6	2	15.6	1	25.5	3	19.8
Mulholland Hwy (CRR)[4]	3	19.8	3	19.8	3	19.8			2	11.6
Circle X Ranch	4	11.6					2	31.4	1	17.9
Danielson Ranch										
La Jolla Valley Walk-in	5	13.8	4	21.2						
Western Terminus	6	5.1	5	5.1	4	25.3	3	17.9		

Note: Mileage includes distances off the BBT to camps (Malibu Creek 1.9 mi, Circle X Ranch 2.1 mi, La Jolla Valley 0.5 mi)
[4] There are several roads between Malibu Creek and Circle X Ranch (31.4 mi) that can be used to access off-trail lodging. Mulholland Highway could be substituted for another one of these roads to alter the distance hiked that day.

B. TCT Planning Tools

Overview Map

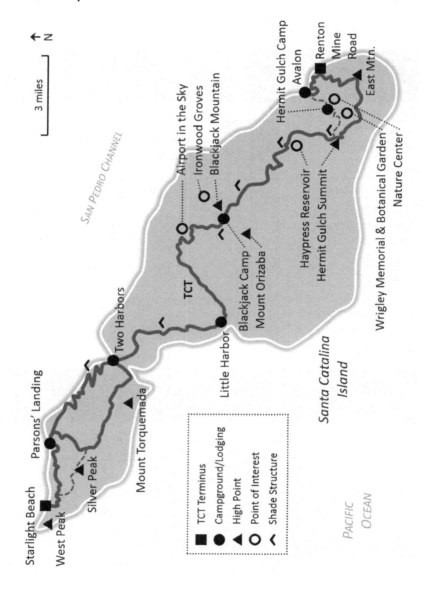

< Appendices >

Elevation Profile

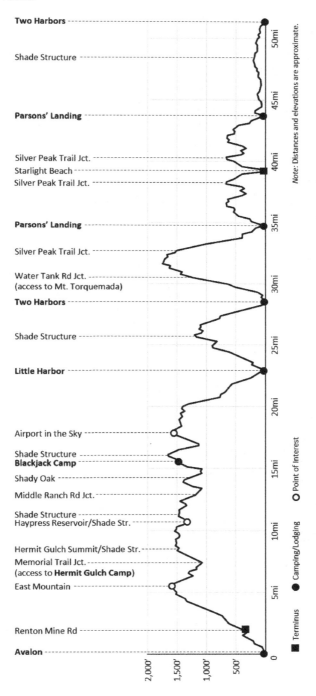

Note: Distances and elevations are approximate.

Two Harbors

Shade Structure

Parsons' Landing

Silver Peak Trail Jct.
Starlight Beach
Silver Peak Trail Jct.

Parsons' Landing

Silver Peak Trail Jct.

Water Tank Rd Jct.
(access to Mt. Torquemada)

Two Harbors

Shade Structure

Little Harbor

Airport in the Sky

Shade Structure
Blackjack Camp

Shady Oak

Middle Ranch Rd Jct.

Shade Structure
Haypress Reservoir/Shade Str.

Hermit Gulch Summit/Shade Str.
Memorial Trail Jct.
(access to **Hermit Gulch Camp)**
East Mountain

Renton Mine Rd

Avalon

50mi
45mi
40mi
35mi
30mi
25mi
20mi
15mi
10mi
5mi
0

2,000'   1,500'   1,000'   500'

O Point of Interest

● Camping/Lodging

■ Terminus

C. BBT Planning Tools

Overview Map

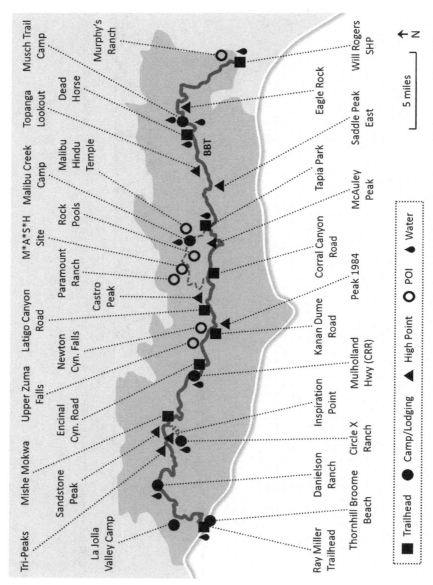

Elevation Profile

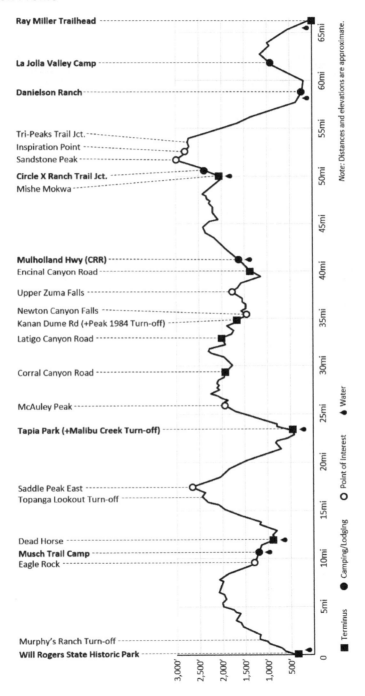

Ray Miller Trailhead

La Jolla Valley Camp

Danielson Ranch

Tri-Peaks Trail Jct.
Inspiration Point
Sandstone Peak
Circle X Ranch Trail Jct.
Mishe Mokwa

Mulholland Hwy (CRR)
Encinal Canyon Road

Upper Zuma Falls

Newton Canyon Falls
Kanan Dume Rd (+Peak 1984 Turn-off)
Latigo Canyon Road

Corral Canyon Road

McAuley Peak

Tapia Park (+Malibu Creek Turn-off)

Saddle Peak East
Topanga Lookout Turn-off

Dead Horse
Musch Trail Camp
Eagle Rock

Murphy's Ranch Turn-off
Will Rogers State Historic Park

Note: Distances and elevations are approximate.

♦ Water

○ Point of Interest

● Camping/Lodging

■ Terminus

65mi 60mi 55mi 50mi 45mi 40mi 35mi 30mi 25mi 20mi 15mi 10mi 5mi 0

3,000' 2,500' 2,000' 1,500' 1,000' 500'

D. Mileage Data Tables

Trans-Catalina Trail

Landmark	Distance (mi)	Cumulative (mi)	Elevation (feet)
Avalon Ferry Terminal	0	0	0
Eastern Terminus – Renton Mine Road Trailhead	1.8	1.8	302
Hermit Gulch Summit Shade Structure	6.4	8.2	1,493
Haypress Reservoir	2.3	10.5	1,319
Blackjack Campground	5.2	15.7	1,512
Trail to Mt. Orizaba (1.1 mi S)	0.3	16.0	1,621
Shade Structure. Trail to Blackjack Mountain (0.8 mi E), Ironwood Groves (1.7 m E)	0.1	16.1	1,657
Airport in the Sky (0.1 mi N)	1.6	17.7	1,555
Little Harbor	5.2	22.9	33
Shade Structure	2.8	25.7	1,207
Two Harbors	2.4	28.1	39
Water Tank Road	2.3	30.4	1,260
Trail to Silver Peak (1.0 mi W), Starlight Beach via Silver Peak (3.7 mi W)	2.2	32.6	1,519
Parsons' Landing	2.1	34.7	13
Trail to Silver Peak (1.7 mi E)	3.6	38.3	676
Route to West Peak (0.6 mi W)	0.4	38.7	512
Western Terminus – Starlight Beach	0.6	39.3	23
Return to Parsons' Landing	4.6	43.9	13
Two Harbors via West End Road	7.5	51.4	39

Backbone Trail

Landmark	Distance (mi)	Cumulative (mi)	Elevation (feet)
Eastern Terminus – Will Rogers SHP	0.0	0.0	433
Trail to Rustic Canyon (0.6 mi E)	1.8	1.8	1,188
The Hub (BBT splits N to Eagle Rock or S to Eagle Spring, rejoins in 1.4 mi)	5.6	7.4	1,990
Eagle Rock	1.0	8.4	1,916
Eagle Junction	0.4	8.8	1,673
Musch Trail Camp via Eagle Rock	1.1	9.9	1,316
Trippet Ranch (0.1 mi S) via Musch Trail Camp	0.9	10.8	1,195
Dead Horse Trailhead at Topanga Canyon Blvd	1.2	12.0	850
Old Topanga Canyon Road	0.8	12.8	774
Stunt Road Overlook	4.1	16.9	2,360
Trail to Saddle Peak (0.2 mi S)	0.7	17.6	2,713
Piuma Road Crossing	4.1	21.7	728
Piuma Rd (WB: W at road, 0.3 mi to Malibu Cyn Rd. EB: S at signed trail.)	1.4	23.1	459
Tapia Park Trailhead (Malibu Creek Campground 1.9 mi N)	0.5	23.6	490
McAuley Peak	2.8	26.4	1,939
Corral Canyon Trailhead	2.5	28.9	1,998
Latigo Canyon Trailhead	4.2	33.1	2,037
Kanan Dume Rd/Newton Cyn Trailhead	2.3	35.4	1,529
Zuma Ridge Trail (PCH 6.1 mi S)	2.6	38.0	1,788
Encinal Canyon Rd Trailhead	2.3	40.3	1,401
Mulholland Highway (CRR)	1.2	41.5	1,621
Yerba Buena Rd	4.4	45.9	2,080
Mishe Mokwa Trailhead	4.6	50.5	2,103
Trail to Circle X Ranch (2.1 mi SW)	0.5	51.0	2,297
Trail to Sandstone Peak (0.1 mi E)	1.1	52.1	2,970
Trail to Tri-Peaks (0.5 mi N)	1.2	53.3	2,648
Trail to Tri-Peaks (0.6 mi N)	0.4	53.7	2,710
Danielson Ranch	5.1	58.8	300
Trail to La Jolla Valley Walk-in Camp (0.5 mi N)	3.4	62.2	932
Western Terminus – Ray Miller Trailhead	4.6	66.8	33

E. Checklists

Clothing

	Hiking shirt
	Hiking shorts
	Hat (sun protection)
	Sunglasses
	Footwear
	Socks
	Thermal top and bottoms

	Light fleece or down jacket
	Rain jacket
	Warm hat
	*Gaiters
	*Camp shoes/flip-flops
	*Underwear

* Optional item

Gear

	Backpack
	Shelter, stakes, ground sheet
	Sleeping bag
	Sleeping pad
	Stove and fuel
	Lighter and matches
	Cookware and utensils
	Water storage
	Food
	Knife
	First aid kit
	Sunblock and lip balm
	Maps/guidebook
	Compass
	ID/money

	Toothbrush and toothpaste
	Hand sanitizer
	Toilet paper
	Head lamp/extra batteries
	Bandana
	*Water treatment
	*Camera and accessories
	*Watch
	*Phone
	*Trekking poles
	*Insect repellent
	*Wet wipes
	*Portable charger
	*Pack cover
	*Hiking umbrella

* Optional item

Food List per Day per Person (3 alternatives per meal)

Breakfast
Instant oatmeal, dried fruit
Pastries or bagels with spread
Breakfast shake with coffee, chocolate, powdered milk

Lunch
Canned, dried, or smoked meat with cheese and crackers
Tuna pouch with tortillas, mayo packet, and seasonings
Peanut butter, jelly, honey with crackers or bread

Snacks
Nuts and seeds
Dried fruit
Protein/granola bars

Dinner
Freeze-dried instant meal
Instant potatoes, bacon bits, olive oil
Rice, cheese, soup packet, tuna or chicken packet

Other Food Items / Condiments

Sugar
Coffee (and creamer)
Powdered milk
Tea
Condiment packets
Powdered drink mixes

Salt and pepper
Herbs and spices
Hot/soy sauce
Parmesan
Olive oil
Chocolate or other treats

F. Food Suggestions

Breakfast

- Oatmeal with dried fruits, sugars, dried coconut, chocolate
- Grits with cheese, hot sauce
- Dry milk, powdered soy, coconut, or almond milk
- Honey buns, pastries, cakes
- Breakfast biscuits
- Cereal bars
- Breakfast shakes (coffee, powdered milk, protein shake, breakfast powders)
- Bagel, english muffin, tortilla, pita
- Almond, cashew or peanut butter
- Chocolate spread, jelly, and honey
- Freeze-dried breakfasts
- Tea, coffee, hot chocolate, sugar

Lunch

- Smoked/dried sausage (summer sausage or salami), beef and other jerkies
- Tuna and salmon in pouches
- Cheese
- Hard-boiled eggs
- Hummus
- Crackers, breads (tortillas, pita, bagels, english muffins)
- Almond, cashew or peanut butter
- Chocolate spread, jelly, and honey
- Olive oil and herbs
- Vegetable spreads
- Prepared sandwich or perishable meal for your first day

Snacks

- Almonds, pistachios, other nuts and seeds
- Dried fruits (mango, apricot, banana, date, fig, apple, cherry, cranberry), fruit leather
- Power bars and gels
- Protein, granola, and cereal bars
- Veggie chips, sun dried tomatoes
- Chips, crackers, pretzels, cookies
- Chocolate, candy bars, chewy candy, fruit snacks
- Powdered drink mixes

Dinner

- Freeze dried instant meals
- Pasta
- Rice
- Quinoa
- Couscous
- Ramen noodles
- Stove top
- Macaroni and cheese
- Instant mashed potatoes
- Burritos (rice, beans, cheese)
- Packaged chicken or tuna
- Beef jerky
- Bacon bits
- Dried vegetables (peas, carrots, peppers, sun dried tomatoes, mushroom)
- Condiments: salt, pepper, herbs, spices, taco seasoning, hot sauce, soy sauce, olive oil, parmesan cheese
- Tea, instant hot chocolate, honey

G. TCT Trail Expansion Program

Below is a summary of the Catalina Island Conservancy's trail expansion program, called *Trekking Catalina*, including descriptions of the three segments of the TCT that could be affected by it.

1) Airport in the Sky to Little Harbor:

Currently, the TCT turns west onto Sheep Chute Road, 1.8 miles from the Airport in the Sky turn off, and follows Sheep Chute Road all the way down to Little Harbor. New single-track trail has been constructed north of and running parallel to Sheep Chute Road on the ridge above Big Springs Canyon that will then connect with an old access road before heading into Little Harbor. Rather than turning west onto Sheep Chute Road from the airport, continue along Empire Landing Road for another 0.5 to 0.7 miles before heading west onto single-track trail. This should smooth out some of the steep climbs for eastbound hikers heading from Little Harbor to the airport. This change could add 0.4 miles to the length of the TCT.

1) Parsons' Landing heading west to Starlight Beach:

0.4 miles west of Parsons' Landing as you head to Starlight Beach, there is a right (west) turn onto a dirt road that drops down quickly into a creek bed before rising again along two large switchbacks. The new route will continue south, past the turn 0.4 miles from Parsons' Landing, on an existing road before contouring back along the hillside to rejoin the West End Road going out to Starlight Beach. This change would only add around 200 feet to the length of the TCT.

3) West End Road near Starlight Beach and Silver Peak Trail:

Probably the biggest improvement to the hiking experience will be to remove a pointless up and down on the west end of the island as you approach Starlight Beach. The West End Road provides emergency and maintenance vehicle access to the remote west end of the island. When the road was washed out years ago, a reroute had to be constructed. The result was a steep drop, then elevation gain in the span of about a mile to go around the washout, which is very frustrating to hikers using their own power to walk the route. The update will make use of available portions of the old road plus new single-track trail to create a direct line for hikers that would avoid this elevation drop. I was able to find the old road on my TCT hike in October of 2016, and even before trail improvements, it was passable. WB hikers turn left onto access road just beyond mile marker

35 at unmarked junction. EB hikers, 0.1 miles east of the Silver Peak Trail junction, as the TCT begins a long decline, look for a path breaking right off TCT onto embankment. The old road is visible on the Catalina Island Conservancy's main TCT map, between mile markers 35 and 36. This should shorten the TCT by about 0.3 miles.

Note:

There are many administrative actions that need to occur for these changes to officially be added to the TCT, such as updating and printing official maps, adding and replacing trail signs, and redoing the mileage markers along the route to reflect the updates. I would recommend taking these new routes even if they are not officially added to the TCT by the time you are hiking. They are put in place to make the hiking experience easier and less confusing, so you might as well take advantage of them. Total additional mileage is estimated at only 0.1 miles. These routes are approximated on my custom CalTopo TCT map and will be updated as the Trekking Catalina trails program develops.

Additional improvements to the Catalina Island trail system include access to Empire Quarry, a Cat Harbor overlook, a connector between the Airport in the Sky and Two Harbors, Eagle's Nest, Cottonwood Canyon, Skull Ridge, Patrick's Reservoir, and Silver Canyon, Lone Tree Road overlooking the dramatic Palisades cliffs on the island's south coastline, and Avalon from the TCT near Stage Road that could be used to shortcut the distance from Avalon to Blackjack Campground or do a longer loop hike of the east end around Avalon.

H. Contact Information

Catalina Island Conservancy
Conservancy House
125 Clarissa Ave
Avalon, CA 90704
+1 (310) 510-2595 x0

Two Harbors Visitor Services
Isthmus Pier
Two Harbors, CA 90704
+1 (310) 510-4205

National Park Service
Santa Monica Mountains Interagency Visitor Center
26876 Mulholland Highway
Calabasas, CA 91302
+1 (805) 370-2301

California State Parks
Angeles District
1925 Las Virgenes Road
Calabasas, CA 91302-1909
+1 (818) 880-0363

I. Links & References

Catalina Island Conservancy

Maps of the TCT and general info on the trail. A good starting point if you are looking for information on non-hiking activities on the island. Their website also contains information on the biology of the island and conservation efforts to preserve rare and native species.

http://www.catalinaconservancy.org
(Visit > Things to Do > Hiking and Biking > Trans-Catalina Trail)

Catalina Island Chamber of Commerce and Visitors Bureau

Information on hotels, activities, travel, and any recreation around Catalina Island you might want to partake in after your hike.

https://www.catalinachamber.com

National Park Service

Maps of the BBT and general info on the trail.

https://www.nps.gov/samo/planyourvisit/backbonetrail.htm

CalTopo

Online map viewer and builder that was a great resource for this book. The map building tools are convenient, extensive, and mostly free. The elevation data and some of the distance data reported in this book were generated using CalTopo.

http://caltopo.com/

Link to custom TCT CalTopo map: *http://caltopo.com/m/G9ES*

Link to custom BBT CalTopo map: *http://caltopo.com/m/D1JH*

Hein, Frank; de la Rosa, Carlos

Comprehensive natural history of Catalina Island, including the rare plant and animal species that inhabit the island.

Wild Catalina Island: Natural Secrets and Ecological Triumphs, The History Press, 2013

McAuley, Milt

An excellent BBT guide, published 26 years before the trail was finally completed. It provides turn-by-turn descriptions, an outstanding overview of the natural history of the trail, and an interesting look at the trails formation over the years.

Guide to the Backbone Trail, Canyon Publishing Company, 1990

McAuley, Milt

Guide that covers the flowers, trees, shrubs, and other plants of the Santa Monica Mountains. Includes photos and descriptions for help with identification out on the trail.

Wildflowers of the Santa Monica Mountains, Canyon Publishing Company, 1996

And, of course, visit:

www.PlanAndGoHiking.com

for more information and pictures.

We look forward to and appreciate your feedback!

@planandgohiking

J. List of Abbreviations

aka	also known as
BBT	Backbone Trail
CG	Campground
CRR	Cleft of the Rock Ranch
Cyn.	Canyon
EB	Eastbound
ETA	Estimated Time of Arrival
ETD	Estimate of Trail Days
NPS	National Park Service
POI	Point of Interest
SHP	State Historic Park
SP	State Park
TCT	Trans-Catalina Trail
TH	Trailhead
WB	Westbound

About the Author

In addition to hiking the Backbone Trail and Trans-Catalina Trail twice each, Sam Ward has backpacked over 7,000 miles along the Appalachian Trail (2008), Pacific Crest Trail (2011), and Continental Divide Trail (2015), aka the Triple Crown, as well as many more as a weekend warrior. He works as an environmental engineer and lives in Los Angeles.

Sam on the Continental Divide in Colorado

Special Thanks

Thank you to those who have worked for decades to establish a continuous footpath through the Santa Monica Mountains and to protect open space around Los Angeles, as well as those working to preserve and restore the delicate ecological balance on Catalina Island. Thank you to Ranger Sheila at the National Park Service, who always answered my weird and specific questions with enthusiasm and grace.

I never would have taken an interest in backpacking were it not for Camp Tohkomeupog in East Madison, NH. They taught me everything I needed to know about trip planning, backcountry ethics, mental toughness, and how to have fun in a whiteout.

Thank you and apologies to everyone I have hiked with over the years. I love you all and learned so much about hiking, travelling, and appreciating time spent in the wilderness. Special shoutout to my brother Ben, who hiked the PCT with me, as we learned on the fly all about desert hiking and snow travel, and my good friend Picker, who hiked the CDT with me and kept me motivated (and alive) along a brutal trail.

Thank you to Yvonne for pushing me in new directions on our hikes and bringing joy with you everywhere we go.

Special thank you to everyone at One Straw Farm for their support while writing this book. Thank you to my family, especially my grandmother Rachel Ward, who took the time to help edit and polish this book.

Thank you to my uncle Tom, who taught me at a young age not to fear nature but to respect it.

Thank you to all my family and friends who sent messages that kept me focused and uplifted while on my thru-hikes. A huge thank you to my parents, Betsy and Gary, whose love and encouragement whenever I decided to head off on a long walk led me to experience life in new and exciting ways.

Disclaimer

The information provided in this book is accurate to the best of author's and publisher's knowledge. However, there is no aspiration, guarantee, or claim to the correctness, completeness, and validity of any information given. Readers should be aware that internet addresses, phone numbers, mailing addresses, as well as prices, services, etc. were believed to be accurate at time of publication, but are subject to change without notice.

References are provided for informational purposes only. Neither author(s) nor the publisher have control over the content of websites, books, or other third party sources listed in this book and, consequently, do not accept responsibility for any content referred to herein. The mention of products, companies, organizations, or authorities in this book does not imply any affiliation with or endorsement by author(s) or publisher, and vice versa. All product and company names are trademarks™ or registered® trademarks of their respective holders.

This book is not a medical guidebook. The information and advice provided herein are merely intended as a reference and explicitly not as a substitute for professional medical advice. Consult a physician to discuss whether or not your health and fitness level are appropriate for the physical activities describe in this book, especially, if you are aware of any pre-existing conditions or issues.

* * *

Made in the USA
Columbia, SC
17 April 2022

59090536R00095